Brett Favre: The Inspiring Story of One of Football's Greatest Quarterbacks

An Unauthorized Biography

By: Clayton Geoffreys

Visit my website at www.claytongeoffreys.com
Cover photo by Mike Morbeck is licensed under CC BY 2.0 / modified from original

Table of Contents

Foreword

If you ask any football fan who grew up in the 90s or early 2000s who was one of the best quarterbacks to play the game, it would not take long before the name Brett Favre was mentioned. Brett "The Gunslinger" Favre, spent two decades in the National Football League, most notably being the face of the Green Bay Packers' franchise for years. As the only player to ever be selected as the Most Valuable Player three consecutive times, Favre left a legacy that puts him in the most elite group of quarterbacks to play football in the modern era. Thank you for purchasing *Brett Favre: The Inspiring Story of One of Football's Greatest Quarterbacks*. In this unauthorized biography, we will learn Brett Favre's incredible life story and impact on the game of football. Hope you enjoy and if you do, please do not forget to leave a review!

Also, check out my website at claytongeoffreys.com to join my exclusive list where I let you know about my latest books. To thank you for your purchase, you can go to my site to download a free copy of *33 Life Lessons: Success Principles, Career Advice & Habits of Successful People*. In the book, you'll learn from some of the greatest thought leaders of different industries on what it takes to become successful and how to live a great life.

Cheers,

Clayton Geoffreys

Visit me at www.claytongeoffreys.com

Introduction

Most football fans know who Brett Favre is: a three-time NFL MVP who is the face of the Green Bay Packers franchise. In fact, when people talk about the Packers, they are sure to bring Favre into the discussion. And who can blame them? He donned the team's Green and Gold colors for 16 seasons. He's one of those quarterbacks whom people associate with just one team (just like Johnny Unitas of the Baltimore Colts, Joe Namath of the New York Jets, and Dan Marino of the Miami Dolphins).

If you had watched Favre all these years, you were amazed at how precise his throws to his receivers were. Some of them even defied logic: How could Favre have eluded several angry linebackers to throw a perfect spiral to the end zone? How could Favre have endured in the challenging National Football League? As you will find out, there's only one answer to that: Hard work.

However, it is much more than that. You may think Favre had it all: an illustrious career, an MVP trophy, admiring fans, and a happy family. To truly appreciate Favre's journey, one has to dig deeper – much deeper. He traces his roots to little-known Kiln, Mississippi, a small town an hour away from New Orleans where Favre honed his legendary football skills. As a child, he had it all – strength, dedication, and the matching work ethic. Favre never wasted his talents. He knew he had what it took to succeed. Nonetheless, he never took anything for granted. You would also be surprised at the several stumbling blocks Favre had to overcome to achieve greatness. Even though he is a famous personality, he is a Mississippi country boy at heart. He is just like any regular person who encounters trials on the journey of life.

However, what sets Favre apart from the rest is his resilience. As you read this book, try to appreciate every single moment he went through. Once you do that, you will have a newfound appreciation for the legend of Brett Lorenzo Favre.

Chapter 1: Childhood and Early Years

Brett Lorenzo Favre was born on October 10, 1969, in Gulfport, Mississippi, to parents Irvin and Bonita. The former was a high school baseball and football coach while the latter was a special education teacher. Brett was their second child behind Scott. Two more kids, Jeff and Brandi, would follow. Brett Favre's heritage included a combination of French, Swiss-German, Spanish, and Choctaw Native American. He was a rare and unique breed regarding his bloodline.

His great-great-great-great-great grandfather from Irvin's side, Simon Favre, was an interpreter and linguist. Brett got his Choctaw Native American blood from Simon's mistress, a woman named Pistikiokonay. His paternal grandparents were Alvin Ernest Favre and Mary A. Spikes. On the other side, his maternal grandparents were Benie Lorenzo French and Izella Garriga. It was on this side of the family that Brett Favre got his Spanish heritage.[i]

He was also no normal baby – he weighed nine pounds and 15 ounces at birth, per the *Milwaukee Journal Sentinel's* Gary D'Amato.[ii] It was evident very early in life he had the makings of an excellent athlete. The doctor even joked Favre was already doing push-ups in the nursery room.[iii]

Irvin Favre, who had the nickname "Irv," reportedly had told his wife Bonita to hurry up delivering their second child because he had to coach his St. John Eagles in a game against the Hancock North Central Hawks. The couple had no idea Brett would suit up for the Hawks 14 years later.

A mutual friend introduced them to each other at a beach party in Henderson Point, Mississippi. They clicked from the get-go. The one thing they had in common was their love for sports: Irv, who was also known as "Chief," played baseball and football. He played baseball in the collegiate and semi-professional ranks. For her part, Bonita was a basketball player. When she didn't notice his cast from a previous football injury was no longer there on Homecoming Day, he became upset. He was so mad he threw his corsage at her. It was a good thing he forgave her. One day, Irv proposed to Bonita on a baseball field, and she said yes. Their romance reached a climax in a most appropriate setting. They would spend many more nights as husband and wife dating on football and baseball fields. No wonder their enthusiasm for sports rubbed off so quickly on their future children.

When Brett was two years old, Irv became the assistant football coach at Hancock North Central High School. He and Bonita also took on physical education teaching jobs at the school. The latter was also a special education teacher, and worked as the lifeguard director in Diamondhead, Mississippi, per Koestler-Grack. For their part, Brett and his brother Scott would dress up as mascots whenever they watched the Hawks play in the stadium.

In November 2004, Bonita Favre told OnMilwaukee.com's Tim Gutowski that her son Brett inherited traits from both her and her husband.

"He's probably got both of us," she said. "He's hard-headed like his dad, though Irv's not here to defend himself (he died due to a heart attack a year earlier). He's got some assets from both of us and some bad points, too. Brett just has a very strong determination, always has. Don't tell him he can't do something because then he's going to tell you he will."[iv]

According to Rachel A. Koestler-Grack, Brett Favre grew up in Kiln, Mississippi, a town with a population of only 2,000 people located 12 miles north of the Gulf of Mexico. There were very few establishments in the town. The downtown area featured a yellow caution light and several offices. Favre described Kiln (pronounced "Kill") as "the kind of place where people work on cars all day, party all night, and wrap it all up with a few bar room brawls," per Koestler-Grack.

Favre and his family lived in a two-bedroom house situated on a 52-acre property. The Kiln Volunteer Fire Department required all of the streets in the town to have a name. The future NFL star and his family came up with a unique one for theirs: "Irvin Favre Drive." Their grandparents, Grandpa French and Grandma French, lived in a nearby trailer. The former owned a bar and restaurant known as "Bennie's French Tavern." On the other hand, Brett affectionately called the latter "Mee-Maw." Koestler-Grack says Favre claimed his Mee-Maw "served the best gumbo, shrimp creole, and red beans and rice on the Gulf Coast." Favre and his brothers would spend a lot of time at their grandpa's tavern; they would either run on the adjacent beachfront or play inside.

Mee-Maw also told her grandson that her husband knew the gangster Al Capone. She also told him his grandpa had met Bonnie and Clyde before a posse of police officers killed them in neighboring Louisiana.

Favre's Aunt Kay lived in a small house next door. Several of his other aunts and uncles also lived within the vicinity. It was a small, tight-knit neighborhood.

The three Favre boys would grow up doing many things together: fishing and swimming in the river, hunting in the forest, and of course, playing sports. D'Amato said they would play football and baseball "on makeshift fields between barns and outbuildings."

In 2005, Jeff Favre told the *Milwaukee Journal Sentinel* he and his brothers grew up in a desolate part of Mississippi. There were hardly any neighbors around. They did not have the luxury of calling other boys so that they could play football or baseball. One of the few playmates they had around was their cousin David Peterson. That made it virtually a sports league comprised of four boys. Despite their lack of numbers, they would always improvise. They resorted to rocks, potatoes, and balls made up of duct tape as their game-day equipment.

Peterson told D'Amato the four of them would go to the barn and throw rocks at one another. Nobody was afraid to get hurt. It was survival of the fittest. When they got home at night, at least one of them would have a new cut, bruise, or scrape. It was a pretty common sight those days. None of them complained one bit. As a matter of fact, they bragged about their achievements. Whether it be a touchdown, home run, or back-breaking play, they would talk about it as soon as they got home. Scott even said they were head and shoulders above everybody else concerning sheer athleticism. After they had used up all of their energy for the day, Bonita Favre would serve them dinner.

She said nobody had a more massive appetite than her boys – they would devour everything in sight.

Brett Favre's penchant for being a prankster and joker began during his childhood. In December 2015, former NFL quarterback and current football television analyst Mark Brunell told CBS Sports' Nate Peterson that Favre and several buddies were once out hunting in the woods when they stumbled upon a deer. They shot it with a .22 rifle, but it survived. After they had shot it, they realized somebody could snitch on them because they had trespassed. They were confused and didn't know what to do – they had to find a way to kill their prey without shooting it. They stumbled upon a puddle and submerged the deer's head into the water until it could no longer breathe. Brunell said it was "one of the funniest stories I've ever heard."[v] Favre would eventually carry on his legacy as a prankster well into his adult years.

He was not just known for his jokes, though. As a youngster, he developed a fascination with alligators. It stemmed from his habit of watching "Tarzan" every Saturday morning, per Koestler-Grack. He and his brothers were not afraid of swimming in the alligator-infested rivers. Favre told *Playboy Magazine's* Kevin Cook in November 1997 that alligators ate four of their dogs. If one lived in Mississippi, it wasn't uncommon at all to find an alligator or two in the nearby swamps. Favre said a 13-foot footer ate one of his family's Labradors named Lucky.[vi]

One day, he and his brothers spotted three alligators in their backyard. He and Scott threw a pack of Oreo cookies in the river and witnessed the alligators go after them. They would see them in their familiar spot after school on a fairly regular basis. According to Favre, if they had no cookies, they would throw the alligators some hot dogs and bread. Sometime soon, their father finally discovered what the commotion was. He grabbed his gun and shot all three alligators on the spot. Brett wasn't so sure if he killed them, though. He said it was tough to kill one with just two or three shots. The only thing he remembered was that all three went back into the water. They never played with the creatures again.

Despite Brett Favre's reputation as a practical joker, he always had dreams of winning a Super Bowl during his childhood. He told Cook he and his brothers would watch NFL football on television every Sunday. They would pretend they were the New Orleans Saints' Archie Manning or the Dallas Cowboys' Roger Staubach.

Favre also looked up to his father Irvin's high school football and baseball players. He also considered them as his heroes. In fact, he also tried chewing tobacco just like his dad and his players. Unfortunately, he said he "got sicker than dog s—t."

Brett Favre told Cook his father was one tough man. Irvin Favre may have had a gruff exterior, but he also allowed his children to learn from their mistakes.

"He's a tough guy, Irvin Favre," Brett told *Playboy Magazine*. "He looks like Sgt. Carter on 'Gomer Pyle.' But he let us sow our oats a little. When I dipped tobacco and threw up, he said, 'That'll teach you.'"

When he and his brothers pushed their father to the limit, the latter gave them a good whipping. Brett Favre said his dad would beat him and his brothers up "with anything from a yardstick to a black rubber hose." He remembered one day when he shot one of his brothers with a BB gun and then hit him on the head with a brick. That same day, he hit his other brother with a baseball bat. Favre did not specify the names of each sibling he victimized. Irvin Favre caught him in the act and gave him the spanking of his life.

Brett admitted his dad's whippings hurt, but he wasn't a crier by nature. When his father spanked him after he had hit his two brothers, he pretended to cry so the beating would stop. His dad finally relented. When he left the room, Brett Favre laughed behind his back.

Even though he managed to pull a fast one on his father occasionally, he said Irvin Favre was tougher on him than his two other brothers. Brett made this admission during an interview for his television documentary entitled "Favre 4ever."[vii]

He told Cook he always had great athleticism, even as a child. He even said he "could break a window from 50 yards." Brett, Scott, and Jeff shared the same pitch-black room. None of them could see the other brothers. It did not faze Brett Favre. They had a weight set near their beds. He would do strength training in the dark. Scott and Jeff laughed at him, but he just shrugged them off.

Brett Favre's first dream was to become a major league pitcher. Remember, he had a great football arm. He also had a great pitching arm – he said he could pitch a fastball in the low 90s. However, his velocity needed a little work. He also admitted he was a terrible basketball player – he couldn't shoot or dribble very well.

In the ensuing years, basketball's loss will prove to be football's biggest gain.

Chapter 2: High School Years

Brett Favre enrolled at Hancock North Central High School. He played baseball and football. When he reached the eighth grade, he earned five varsity letters with the baseball team. Brett's brother, Scott, told *The Milwaukee Journal Sentinel* he was probably the second best player after him. He once doubled in his first at-bat and then homered in his second. In his third at-bat, there were men on all three bases. The opposing manager wanted the pitcher to walk Favre. When the fourth pitch came, Favre managed to hit it over the right-field fence for a ground-rule double. He also earned a reputation for having a blazing fastball when he pitched on the mound. He once knocked another kid to the ground after he had hit him on the helmet with his fastball. Other players would cry and complain about Favre. His pitching arm was notorious.

As a high school football player, he played multiple positions. These included quarterback, lineman, strong safety, placekicker, and punter. However, he did not see much time on the defensive end. His head coach – who also happened to be his father – wanted him and his two brothers to play quarterback.

"Dad was hard on everybody, old school." Jeff Favre told *The Milwaukee Journal Sentinel's* Gus D'Amato in 2005. "He'd run a lot of people off the team. He didn't put up with much (expletive), that's for sure."

Irvin Favre was a big admirer of former Alabama Crimson Tide head football coach Paul "Bear" Bryant. He attended one of his coaching clinics in the early 1970s. When he returned to Hancock North Central High School, he implemented Bryant's wishbone offense – a system which was predicated more on the running game. Passing became an option only when it was necessary. Because of this, Brett Favre rarely threw more than five passes when he played high school football, per D'Amato.

Nonetheless, Favre showed dedication no other high school athlete in Mississippi did.

Remember, this was a youngster who lifted weights in a dark room he shared with his two brothers. When he reached high school, he would do strength training three or four times a week in the offseason. He had also practiced throwing the football by himself or with his then-girlfriend Deanna Tynes as his receiver, per *The Milwaukee Journal Sentinel.*

Chapter 3: College Years at Southern Mississippi

Going into his college years, Brett Lorenzo Favre was not a high-profile recruit like most of his contemporaries. Guys like Russell Maryland (Miami Hurricanes), Eric Turner (UCLA Bruins), Bruce Pickens (Nebraska Cornhuskers), and Todd Lyght (Notre Dame Fighting Irish) were able to join big-name college football programs. Not Brett Favre, the 18-year-old from little-known Kiln, Mississippi.

Favre *told Sports Illustrated's* Leigh Montville on August 23, 1993, that nobody wanted him when he reached the collegiate football ranks.

"I've always had to struggle for what I've got," he said. "I was never recruited for college. No one really wanted me. Coming down here, nobody knows who you are. Three days before the signing date, I was going to either Pearl River Junior College or Delta State. Southern Miss took me as a defensive back. When I went there as a freshman, I worked out both ways at first. I was the seventh quarterback on the depth chart." [viii]

Favre enrolled in Southern Miss in 1987. He got the program's last football scholarship after the intended recipient never showed up.[ix] He added that Southern Miss was a place for misfits. Players who received rejection letters from other schools wound up on the Golden Eagles' roster – if they were lucky. Former Southern Miss assistant sports information director Chuck Bennett confirmed that Signing Day in the school was a long way off from those of the collegiate football powerhouses. He even said he never remembered the Golden Eagles signing any All-Americans during his tenure in the athletics department.[x]

Every time Southern Miss went up against bigger-name teams such as the Alabama Crimson Tide or Auburn Tigers, writers would discuss how other schools turned down Golden Eagles players in their sports columns. If the Golden Eagles pulled off a massive upset, they would holler on the field and let reporters know they were no misfits. Favre and his teammates played the role of underdogs, and they savored every moment.

As the 1987 NCAA football season was about to begin, Bennett recalled that nobody had an idea of who Brett Favre was – even the athletic staff had no clue. Nonetheless, Favre worked his way up to third on the quarterback depth chart as his freshman year kicked off. The unheralded kid from Hancock North Central High School already took the field in the second half of his second college football game. He even had his cheering section for the match. Family members in attendance had worn gold "Favre" t-shirts. It served as ample motivation for Favre – he threw two touchdown passes in the second half to help the Golden Eagles beat the Tulane Green Wave, 31-24.

Favre had a chance to turn heads on his 18th birthday on October 10, 1987, when Southern Miss faced the mighty Florida State Seminoles. The opposing home fans ridiculed him by singing a sarcastic "Happy Birthday" song in a 61-10 blowout loss, per *Sports Illustrated.* Favre just shrugged it off. For him, it was no big deal. He just wanted to do his best every time he was on the field.

According to Bennett, Favre had an "up and down" freshman year at Southern Miss. The latter finished with 1,264 yards, 15 touchdowns, and 13 interceptions in 11 games with the Golden Eagles in 1987.[xi]

Southern Miss experienced a coaching change after Favre's freshman season. Head football coach Jim Carmody resigned on December 3, 1987. Athletics director hired former Texas A&M Aggies assistant Curley Hallman as his replacement two weeks later, per the school's official athletics website.[xii]

Favre had a lot of adjustments to make in his sophomore year – in addition to his new head coach, he also had to adjust to a new offensive line. His five offensive linemen – the players who had to protect him at all costs – were new. Bennett said this group had at least one freshman. Brett Favre had his work cut out for him.

He performed very well in 1988 for the Golden Eagles. So much so, Bennett thought it was his "best year at Southern Miss." On September 24, 1988, Favre showed everyone how talented of a quarterback he was. In a 45-42 win over the East Carolina Pirates, he set up the winning field goal with a 40-yard pass to Golden Eagles wide receiver Alfred Williams at the opponent's 10-yard line. Favre later dubbed it "the hardest ball I had ever thrown," per SouthernMiss.com.

Favre recorded 16 touchdowns and just five interceptions, a noticeable drop-off from the 13 picks he had a year earlier. As a result, Southern Miss won nine of its 11 games in 1988. The two losses were to nationally-ranked teams, the Auburn Tigers and the Florida State Seminoles. What made the feat seem even more daunting was the fact the Golden Eagles played only four home games in Hattiesburg, Miss.

Favre had his usual cheering section every time the Golden Eagles were in Hattiesburg. Each member of the group would wear a shirt identifying who he or she was. For instance, Bonita Favre wore "Brett Favre's Mom" and so on, per Bennett.

Because of Southern Miss' stellar regular-season performance, they received an invite to play in the 1988 Independence Bowl against the UTEP Miners – the school's first bowl game in seven years. The last time the Golden Eagles played in such a game was in 1981 when then-head football coach Bobby Collins led them to that season's Tangerine Bowl. Brett Favre had officially arrived. Because networks were going to air the 1988 Independence Bowl before a national television audience, he had a chance to show everybody what he could do.

The Miners wrote a rap song which insulted the Golden Eagles, and Favre and Co. were not very happy about it. In Bennett's words, "Brett liked to shy away from the limelight, but don't ever try to show him up."

On December 23, 1988, a fired up Southern Miss team ran all over UTEP in the 1988 Independence Bowl, 38-18. Punt return specialist James Henry (who was also a defensive back, and later earned Offensive and Defensive Player of the Game honors) scored two touchdowns in the third quarter while Favre passed for another in the romp – the second bowl game victory in the Golden Eagles' football history. The whole country got a taste of what Brett Favre could do.

Chuck Bennett, Southern Miss' assistant sports information director, kept in touch regularly with Favre's father, Irvin. The latter always wanted more publicity for his son. However, Brett Favre never placed importance on this. Bennett also wanted more people to know about the Golden Eagles' quarterback and the football program in general. As a matter of fact, he told his athletics director, Bill McLellan, he was interested in spearheading a "Brett 4 Heisman" campaign. McLellan initially laughed it off and then screamed at Bennett when he realized he was serious. McLellan eventually relented, but told Bennett he and his staff had to generate enough revenue.

Bennett explained his idea to Irvin Favre. The elder Favre was excited, to say the least. They reached out to the local Miller Beer distributor, who agreed to be one of their sponsors. As the summer of 1989 approached, the Southern Miss athletics department sent out news and notes about Favre. Bennett was no longer satisfied with local and statewide attention – he wanted national publicity for his quarterback and the program. He wanted to put Southern Miss football on the map. Brett Favre would be at the focal point.

Bennett and Co. ran into several obstacles. The biggest one was a lack of exposure – the Golden Eagles rarely appeared on national television. Nobody really knew who they were. As the 1989 season opener against Florida State drew nearer, Southern Miss received more publicity. Bennett recalled collecting several national newspaper and magazine clippings mentioning the program. Remember, there was no Internet at this time. For the Golden Eagles to be cited in those publications had to be a very big deal.

The 1989 NCAA football season officially kicked off on September 2 against the Seminoles. It was initially a home game for the Golden Eagles. However, the city of Jacksonville, Florida, offered $500,000 for the opportunity to host the game, per the Golden Eagles' official athletics website. WTBS aired the game. It was just the second television appearance for Favre, who was barely 20 years old. He was clutch in this one – he threw a two-yard touchdown pass to tight end Anthony Harris with just 23 seconds remaining to secure the improbable 26-23 upset over Florida State.

Once the final whistle blew, Bennett said: "the phones rang off the hook." He went straight back to Hattiesburg to work the phone lines even before the rest of the team returned. Southern Miss shot up to 20th in the national football rankings. Before that, the Golden Eagles had never been in ESPN's Top 20 poll. The last time they had made it to an *Associated Press* ranking was eight years earlier. To top it all off, a CNN newscaster held up a "Brett 4 Heisman" bumper sticker in front of a national television audience. The anchor described Favre as "the best player you have never heard of." For Bennett, it was a huge step in the right direction for his quarterback and the football program.

The campaign gathered even more steam when *The Sporting News* rang up Bennett to inform him that the publication had selected Favre as one of the five football players it would highlight on its college football radio show on Tuesday of the following week. *The Sporting News* was no ordinary sports media outlet – it was one of the top in the country. Favre was now in the national media spotlight. Bennett worked with Favre frantically to prepare him for this all-important interview. The Golden Eagles quarterback had an opportunity to be the unofficial spokesperson for his football program.

Alas, he was a no-show.

Bennett said Favre hung out with a few of his buddies and "blew off the interview." The Southern Miss assistant sports media director was steaming – his quarterback had a chance to give his football team more recognition, and he blew it.

It was about to get worse for the Golden Eagles.

They were set to take on their powerful in-state rivals, the Mississippi State Bulldogs, at their MM Roberts Stadium the following week. The game had a fascinating sub-plot. The Bulldogs' defensive coordinator was none other than Southern Miss' former head football coach, Jim Carmody.

As fate would have it, the Golden Eagles lost, 26-23. Their fans hated Mississippi State with a passion. For them to see their rivals carry their former head football coach off the field made it even worse, per Bennett.

Southern Miss then lost three consecutive games to fall 1-4 on the season. They were a far cry from the 20th-ranked team they were after the Florida State conquest. Bennett remembered attendance dipped dramatically at each home game. Bear in mind a typical college football game averages around fifty thousand people or so. At the East Carolina Pirates game, only 11,189 Golden Eagles fans turned up.

Two weeks after the loss to Mississippi State, Southern Miss took on the Louisville Cardinals. Favre played a crucial role in a game sports aficionados dubbed "The Miracle of Louisville." He threw a desperate Hail Mary pass in the waning moments of the match. Golden Eagles wide receiver Michael Jackson (who later played for the NFL's Cleveland Browns and Baltimore Ravens) tipped the pass. Teammate Daryl Tillman managed to catch it and then galloped into the end zone as time expired. Final score: Southern Miss 16, Louisville 10.

Unfortunately for the Golden Eagles, moments like that were few and far between.

In his junior season, Favre threw for 2,588 yards, 14 touchdowns, and ten interceptions. Southern Miss won just five games in 1989. Brett Favre may have earned some recognition, but it all went for naught as his team tumbled down the standings.

Despite that, Favre gained a reputation for his fearlessness on the field as his senior season approached, per *Sports Illustrated's* Leigh Montville. Even better, NFL scouts began to set their sights on him. One of them happened to be Buffalo Bills vice president and general manager, Bill Polian. When he returned from a trip to scout Favre, team owner Ralph Wilson asked him if he found any outstanding players. "I just saw the next great quarterback," Polian quipped.[xiii]

And then the unthinkable happened.

In July 1990, Favre was on his way home from a fishing trip to Ship Island. Blinded by the lights of an oncoming car, his vehicle swerved, hit some gravel, and flipped over. His brother Scott had followed him on a convoy. He told Montville that one of his brother's flips was so high "you could have driven a dump truck underneath the car." Brett's car then hit a tree. Scott then smashed his brother's car window with a golf club so he could pull him out. The Golden Eagles quarterback had a concussion, lacerations, and a cracked vertebra.

"I was out of the hospital, and I thought I was okay," Brett Favre told *Sports Illustrated* on August 23, 1993. "I wasn't eating much, though, and when I did, I was throwing up. I kept having these abdominal pains, and they started to get worse. I went back to the hospital, and they found (out) that a lot of my intestines had died."

Surgeons removed approximately 30 inches of intestine from Favre. When he reported for summer camp in August, he still had problems eating. He went back to Kiln, where his grandmother Mee-Maw whipped up delicious Mississippi-style dishes for him.

In the aftermath of Favre's accident, Southern Miss head football coach Curly Hallman and his staff kept things under the radar – they refused to divulge any valuable information regarding their quarterback's playing status. Assistant sports information director Chuck Bennett recalled Favre trying to discuss anything related to his accident in July.

Favre eventually suited up for the Golden Eagles five weeks after his intestinal surgery. He was 30 pounds underweight. A skinnier Favre led the Golden Eagles to a 27-24 upset victory over the 13th-ranked Alabama Crimson Tide on September 8, 1990. His heroics spoiled the debut of new Alabama head football coach Gene Stallings, per the Southern Miss' official athletics website.

Stallings shrugged it off. Instead, he paid the Golden Eagles' quarterback a major compliment.

"You can call it a miracle, or a legend, or whatever you want to," he told *Sports Illustrated*. "I just know on that day, Brett Favre was larger than life."

Stallings' words were prophetic – Favre led Southern Miss to an 8-3 win-loss record in 1990. It was a three-game improvement from the year before. If it were a college basketball season, it would have represented a 15-game turnaround.

Toward the end of the 1990 NCAA football season, Curly Hallman resigned to become the new head football coach of the LSU Tigers. Bennett said the Golden Eagles' key victories over the Alabama Crimson Tide and Auburn Tigers that year made Hallman a hot coaching commodity. He just could not pass up an offer coming from a SEC powerhouse such as LSU. The Southern Miss athletics director tapped former Golden Eagles quarterback, Jeff Bower, to be his new head football coach on December 2, 1990, per the school's official athletics website.

Bower called the shots for Southern Miss in the All-American Bowl against the North Carolina State Wolfpack in Birmingham, Alabama on December 28, 1990. Favre threw for 341 yards, a Southern Miss bowl-game record. However, the Wolfpack prevailed, 31-27, in Brett Lorenzo Favre's last college football game.

Favre may have had his moments in 1990, but he "never was 100 percent recovered from the surgery," per Montville. Nonetheless, he also suited up in the Senior Bowl and the East-West Shrine Game.

When Favre had that horrible car accident almost seven months earlier, many pro scouts dropped him from consideration. New York Jets scout Ron Wolf was one of the exceptions – he liked what he saw in Favre during the East-West Shrine Game. He was impressed with how Favre threw the football and, more importantly, with his leadership skills. Wolf noticed how the 21-year-old quarterback made everyone in the huddle listen to him. Not too many college quarterbacks could command that kind of attention.

The Jets weren't able to draft Favre, however. They had already lost their No. 1 draft pick by signing Syracuse Orangemen wide receiver Rob Moore in the supplemental draft, per *Sports Illustrated.* Ironically, Favre would suit up in Jets green in 2008 – 18 years after they first set their sights on him.

After Favre had played his last down for Southern Miss, he prepared for the 1991 NFL Draft. Even in his early 20s, he already had a fascination for golf – Bennett said this was one of Favre's favorite pastimes in the months leading up to the draft.

Brett Lorenzo Favre had already paid his dues in the collegiate ranks. He was ready to take his game to the next level – the National Football League.

Chapter 4: Brett Favre's Professional Career

1991 NFL Draft

Brett Favre rose from complete obscurity to become a hot quarterback commodity in the NFL. Nobody had any idea who he was when he signed with the Southern Miss Golden Eagles as the seventh quarterback on their depth chart in 1987. He let his game do most of the talking. Southern Miss grabbed every possible opportunity to promote Favre and its football program. Three years after Favre became a Golden Eagle, NFL scouts began to salivate at the prospect of signing him. His freak car accident in the summer of 1990 forced some of them to back out. Nevertheless, he remained confident that he was the best quarterback prospect in the 1991 NFL Draft.

The draft took place at the Marriott Marquis in New York City on Sunday, April 21, 1991. That year, the Dallas Cowboys made Miami Hurricanes defensive tackle Russell Maryland the first overall pick.

Favre did not go to New York City. He remained in his house in Mississippi, staying close to the telephone and hoping for a team's general manager to inform him of his selection.

According to WLOX.com's A.J. Giardina, the Favre compound was teeming with people on this Sunday afternoon.[xiv] Remember, Brett Favre had his own cheering section every time his Southern Miss Golden Eagles team played at home. This time, he had a massive cheering section right in the comfort of his home. He always had his loved ones cheering him on.

The Seattle Seahawks made the San Diego State Aztec's Dan McGuire the first quarterback chosen when they drafted 16th overall. Eight picks later, the Los Angeles Raiders made USC Trojans star Todd Marinovich the second quarterback drafted.

Brett Favre's big moment came when the Atlanta Falcons drafted him 33rd overall. He was the sixth pick of the second round.

Even if Favre wasn't the first quarterback drafted in 1991, he remained unfazed. He told Giardina he was the best signal caller that year. All he needed was a bit of time to prove his bold statement.

"Well, we'll see in the coming years who is the best quarterback," he said. "I think I'll prove, you know. I'll prove to everyone that I am the best."

His prophecy would come true several years later.

1991 NFL Season

Brett Favre had made it. He was finally a bona fide NFL quarterback. He agreed to a three-year, $1.4 million rookie deal with the Falcons on July 19, 1991. The contract reportedly included a $350,000 signing bonus.

If Favre had dreams of becoming a star rookie quarterback with the Falcons, he had another thing coming.

The Milwaukee Journal Sentinel's Tom Silverstein dubbed Favre "a whipping boy" in Falcons head coach Jerry Glanville's system. Glanville did not approve of Atlanta vice president of player personnel Ken Herock's decision to draft Favre. The Falcons head coach disliked Favre so much that he said only a plane crash would make him put the rookie quarterback into the game. Falcons offensive coordinator June Jones did not like Favre, either. He and Glanville wanted Louisville Cardinals quarterback Browning Nagle.[xv]

For his part, Favre wasn't dumb – he knew his head coach disliked him. Because of that, he rebelled and refused to follow any of Glanville's rules. Herock admitted to Silverstein that Favre had "a big ego." He thought that he was better than Falcons Pro Bowl quarterback Chris Miller.

Glanville never saw it that way. He refused to give Miller's backup spot to Favre. As a result, Herock was forced to trade for Billy Joe Tolliver. Herock thought all along that the trade would make Glanville soften his stance on Favre. It did not.

With Tolliver on board and Glanville in command, Brett Favre slid to third on the Falcons' quarterback depth chart. His rookie season in Atlanta had become a nightmare.

It grew even worse for Favre. Washington Redskins linebacker Andre Collins intercepted the very first NFL pass he threw and returned it 15 yards for a touchdown on November 10, 1991. The Redskins blew out the Falcons, 56-17. Favre went 0-for-4 passing with two interceptions in the loss.[xvi]

He finished his rookie year with that same stat line, playing in just two games. The other one was against the Los Angeles Rams on October 27, 1991. He never even threw a single pass attempt in that match.[xvii]

It seemed Brett Favre's prospect of blossoming as an Atlanta Falcons quarterback was very bleak, to say the least.

Trade to the Green Bay Packers

Brett Favre suffered through a forgettable rookie season with the Atlanta Falcons. It was anybody's guess if he was going to remain with the team.

It didn't take long for Favre to know what his fate was.

Ron Wolf, the New York Jets scout who developed a liking for the quarterback after his senior season at Southern Miss in 1990, became the Green Bay Packers' general manager on November 27, 1991. He was still with the Jets when the Falcons selected Favre 33rd overall in the 1991 NFL Draft. The Jets had the 34th pick. Had Atlanta not chosen Brett Favre, it was almost a sure thing he would have wound up in New York.

Despite losing out on Favre, Wolf swore he would someday acquire Favre, per Silverstein. His infatuation for the signal caller grew even more when Favre impressed at a scrimmage game between the Atlanta Falcons and Seattle Seahawks in the summer of his rookie year. As Packers general manager, Wolf knew about the beleaguered quarterback's situation with the Falcons.

Rumors had it Wolf had gotten another break before his Packers took on the Falcons in Atlanta on December 1, 1991, just four days after Green Bay hired him to be their new general manager.

Falcons vice president of player personnel Ken Herock, the same executive who had drafted Favre almost eight months earlier, told Wolf in the press box that his only possible chance of seeing Favre throw was several hours before the game. Apparently, Atlanta head coach Jerry Glanville refused to allow Favre to throw during pre-game warm-ups. According to *The Milwaukee Journal Sentinel*, Wolf couldn't make it down to the field because he couldn't get past a massive media throng. It could have been his chance to look at Brett Favre one more time before finalizing a deal for him. The truth was that Wolf already wanted Favre the moment he saw him play in the Portland scrimmage game. Heron's offer to take a look at Favre told Wolf his Atlanta counterpart was open to trade, per Silverstein.

From there on out, Wolf kept in touch with Herock four or five days a week to make sure the Falcons knew about the Packers' interest. His plan was to surrender the second of two first-round draft picks, but he never told Herock about it. All he told the Atlanta executive was the most he would ever give up for Favre was a second-round draft choice, per Silverstein.

Herock had difficulties dealing Favre somewhere else. He met with Glanville, Jones, vice president of football operations Taylor Smith, and the latter's father, Falcons owner Rankin M. Smith, Jr. All of them expressed their sentiments on Brett Favre.

Herock told everyone that he would try to get a first-round pick in exchange for him.

Silverstein talks between the two sides intensified in February. According to ESPN's Rob Demovsky, Favre was at his parents' kitchen in Kiln, Mississippi with his brother Scott when he found out the Falcons traded him to the Packers for a first-round draft pick on February 11, 1992. Atlanta offensive coordinator June Jones – whom Favre had a good relationship with – informed him about the deal.

Nearly 23 years after the historic trade, Favre told Demovsky in a telephone interview that he thought Jones tried to pull a prank. He was also shocked at what he heard. It was no joke. He was heading north to frigid Green Bay, Wisconsin.

"I was kind of shocked," Favre said. "I wondered if this was for real or a joke. He (Jones) said, 'I wish you the best. I enjoyed working with you. I hope you have a great career. This is a great opportunity for you.'"[xviii]

Favre didn't have enough time to absorb Jones' words when he received another phone call. It was his new general manager, Ron Wolf.

"He said, 'Look, I'm the GM in Green Bay,'" Favre told ESPN. "'And we just traded for you, and I want you to know that we're very excited about having you and having you lead our team.'"

Brett Lorenzo Favre's rookie year with the Atlanta Falcons was something he wouldd rather forget. However, it seemed that fate had worked behind the scenes. His nightmarish stint in Atlanta proved to be a brief one. He was now a member of the Green Bay Packers, a team which had produced the likes of Vince Lombardi, Bart Starr, Ray Nitschke, and Paul Hornung. It was also a squad known for their winning ways, having 13 league titles to their credit. The last one came in 1967, just a year after the famous AFL-NFL merger.

It had been 25 years since the Packers last won a title. Green Bay fans wanted another one, and Favre was about to become a centerpiece in reliving the team's lost glory.

1992 NFL Season

Brett Favre had his first training camp with the Green Bay Packers in the summer of 1992. He remained confident as ever.

The Milwaukee Journal's (now known as *The Milwaukee Journal Sentinel*) Bob McGinn asked Favre if he had the physical talent to compete at the level Dan Marino, John Elway,

Troy Aikman, and even Jeff George had. Favre was nonchalant, saying he "could do anything they can do."[xix]

Favre didn't like the fact he was still a backup quarterback heading into his second pro season. He had wanted to be a starter all along. He told McGinn he was ready to assume that role as soon as Packers head coach Mike Holmgren and general manager Ron Wolf felt he could. Favre's leadership and work ethic had impressed Holmgren – he said the new kid on the block could carve a solid niche for himself in the league if he kept it up.

Favre had his work cut out for him. If he wanted to be the starting quarterback, he had to displace Don Majkowski. The projected backup, Mike Tomczak, had held out, per McGinn. It meant the worst-case scenario for Favre was to be a backup in his first season in Green Bay. He said he had nothing personal against Majkowski, whom he respected a great deal. With the latter's recent injury history, Favre felt he would get a chance to play regularly. Once he became the starter, he said it would be that way for quite some time.

"Once I'm in, it's going to be over," he told McGinn. "I really believe it. Just like college."

Favre also felt the sharp contrast in how the Atlanta Falcons and Green Bay Packers went about their business on the field. In one instance, Packers offensive tackle Tony Mandarich walked up to Favre and put his arm around him. They never spoke. However, actions spoke louder than words in that instance. Favre told *The Milwaukee Journal* that "that never happened in Atlanta." Because of that, he said he would play harder than he ever had.

He had to. He confessed to McGinn he was still trying to get a feel for the Packers' offense. In a recent scrimmage, Favre ran around the backfield on five pass plays or so.

Green Bay Packers quarterbacks coach Steve Mariucci said that Favre completed 42 percent of his passes in mini-camps. He improved to 75 percent once training camp kicked off. Mariucci was impressed, though he felt that Favre should improve his decision-making skills.

It didn't take Brett Favre very long to prove that he belonged in the National Football League.

On September 20, 1992, Majkowski sprained the ligaments in his left ankle during the first quarter of a game against the Cincinnati Bengals. Team physicians predicted he would be out for the next two to four weeks, per *Sports Illustrated's* Leigh Montville.

Enter Favre.

He wound up throwing for 289 yards and two touchdowns in an exciting 24-23 win over the Bengals. Favre also showed how clutch of a quarterback he was when he threw the game-winning touchdown pass to wide receiver Kitrick Taylor with just 13 seconds left.[xx]

On July 13, 2015 – nearly 23 years after that magical moment – Favre told ESPN's Rob Demovsky his first game as Packers quarterback was one he will not soon forget.

"The first game I ever played in, in my opinion, gets overlooked probably way more than it should," he said. "How can I not put that high on the list? It was ugly, but so beautiful at the same time."[xxi]

Favre was right. As soon as he took over as Green Bay's quarterback, there was no looking back. Majkowski never became the starter again.

Favre turned heads during the 1992 NFL season. He finished with 3,227 yards, 18 touchdowns, and 13 interceptions.[xxii] According to Montville, he finished sixth in the NFL in completion percentage (64.1). Not bad for an unheralded quarterback who never made an impact the year before.

More impressively, Favre orchestrated a five-game turnaround for the Packers, who were just 4-12 in 1991. Under his leadership, Green Bay improved to 9-7. To top it all off, he also made his first Pro Bowl appearance. Although the team missed the postseason, things looked very rosy for the millions of Cheeseheads (as Packers fans are known) the world over.

1993 NFL Season

Entering his third NFL season, Brett Favre was officially the starting quarterback for the Green Bay Packers, and life on the field could not have been any better. With him under center, Packers head coach Mike Holmgren and Co. wanted to end the team's futility. The last time Green Bay made the postseason was in 1982. That year, they lost to the Dallas Cowboys, 37-26, in the second round of the playoffs. Brett Favre was barely 13 years old then.

Eleven years later, he was the undisputed leader of the Packers' offense. He got off to a good start when he converted 19 of 29 pass attempts for 264 yards and one touchdown in a 36-6 rout of the Los Angeles Rams in Week 1.[xxiii]

The Packers then lost three straight games by an average of nine points each. Opposing defenses managed to keep him in check during that span. He managed just two touchdown passes and threw four interceptions.

Favre and his teammates then turned things around. From October 10 to November 28, the Packers won six of seven games to improve to 7-4 on the 1993 NFL season. On October 24, Favre had his best game of the year. He threw for 268 yards and four touchdowns in a 37-14 road win over the Tampa Bay Buccaneers.

Green Bay had an opportunity to gain more momentum as the season wore on, but faded down the stretch. The team lost three of their last five games to finish the season at 9-7 – the same record as the year before. Favre regressed in his second year as starting quarterback. He did throw for 19 touchdown passes, but also threw for 24 interceptions. He accounted for 30 of the team's 34 turnovers in 1993, per *Sports Illustrated's* Peter King.

"I struggled and I struggled for a long time," Favre told King. "But think about it. I got thrown into the toughest offense in the game as a starter at 22. Every other guy who's played it sat for a year or two and learned. Joe Montana sat behind Steve DeBerg. Steve Young sat behind Joe. Steve Bono sat behind both of them. Ty Detmer and Mark Brunell sat behind me. That's why it was frustrating when people would get on me."

Despite Favre's struggles, two historical moments occurred in the Packers' 1993 NFL season.

The first was the birth of the famous "Lambeau Leap," a feat where a Packers player would dive into the stands after he scored a touchdown. Favre would throw many passes over the years to an assortment of teammates who whooped it up with the fans after a score.

Ironically, a defensive player – strong safety LeRoy Butler – started it all. On December 26, 1993, Butler caused one of the then-Los Angeles Raiders (now the Oakland Raiders) to fumble. Green Bay defensive end Reggie White scooped up the football. As a Raiders player closed in to tackle White, he flipped the ball to Butler for a touchdown – his very first. He dived into the Lambeau stands and celebrated with the Cheeseheads.[xxiv]

The other major accomplishment in Favre's second year as a starter was ending a 10-year playoff drought. The Packers' 9-7 record placed them third in the NFC North and earned them the sixth seed in the conference. Brett Favre would get a taste of postseason football in just his third NFL season. He and his teammates faced the third-seeded Detroit Lions in the 1993

Wild Card Game on January 8, 1994. Detroit beat Green Bay, 30-20, in the two teams' final regular-season games on January 2, 1994. Favre, who was named to his second consecutive Pro Bowl berth, threw four interceptions in the loss.

Six days later, he more than made up for it. Favre proved his first game as the Packers' starting quarterback against the Cincinnati Bengals in 1992 was no fluke. He led Green Bay to an improbable 28-24 road win at the Lions' Pontiac Silverdome – the Packers' first postseason victory since 1982. Detroit led, 24-21, with 2:26 left. After Green Bay had stopped Lions star running back Barry Sanders on his team's 29-yard line, the Packers moved the sticks methodically. Favre threw a 40-yard touchdown pass to wide receiver Sterling Sharpe with 55 seconds remaining to seal the victory. Both Packers head coach Mike Holmgren and quarterbacks coach Steve Mariucci lauded Favre's effort. Any inexperienced quarterback would have gotten rattled in that situation, but not Favre. He led Green Bay's hurry-up offense efficiently under so much pressure.

Packers general manager Ron Wolf, the same man who defied the odds by trading for Favre, told *The Milwaukee Journal's* Bob McGinn on January 8, 1994, that the quarterback was The Chosen One.

"We've put our future in his hands," Wolf beamed. "If that young quarterback read everything written about him, I don't know if he'd make an appearance other than in disguise."[xxv]

Next up for the Packers were the defending Super Bowl champions, the Dallas Cowboys. It was Brett Favre vs. Troy Aikman. Barely two years after the fiasco in Atlanta, Favre was in a position to upset Aikman and Co.

It did not happen.

Favre was relatively quiet in the first half. During that stretch, Dallas scored two touchdowns courtesy of wide receiver Alvin Harper and tight end Jay Novacek to lead, 17-3, at the half. The Cowboys enjoyed their biggest lead of the game when Aikman threw a 19-yard touchdown pass to wide receiver Michael Irvin in the third quarter. At that point, Dallas was up 24-3. Favre recorded two touchdown passes to Robert Brooks and Sterling Sharpe, but it was too little, too late. Final score: Cowboys 27, Packers 17.[xxvi]

Green Bay's 1993 NFL season may have ended on a sour note, but the team made great strides. Nobody expected the Packers to reach the NFC Divisional Round. With a more experienced Brett Favre at quarterback, they were going to reach new heights in 1994.

1994 NFL Season

Brett Favre gave Green Bay Packers fans a taste of what he could do as their starting quarterback. Not only that, he led the Pack to their first playoff win since 1982. The team advanced to the 1993 NFC Divisional Round. They were aiming higher in the 1994 NFL season.

However, the Packers got off to a slow start. They won just three of their first seven games. During that stretch, Favre had nine touchdown passes and seven interceptions – not a very good touchdown-to-interception ratio. It was evident he had not yet shaken off his penchant for making careless plays. Hard evidence of this was the 24 interceptions he threw the season before. Opposing defenses still had the better of Favre – they knew how to read him like a book. After all, he was just in his fourth NFL season. He still had a lot to learn about playing quarterback at the game's highest level.

Green Bay head coach Mike Holmgren had ragged Favre throughout the 1993 season and the first seven games of the following season, per *Sports Illustrated's* Peter King. Holmgren felt Favre was not aiming high enough – he was content with where the Packers were.

"He deserved it, believe me," Holmgren told King on January 27, 1997. "He would say things to me like, 'Hey, we're 9-7, and we made the playoffs. That's a pretty good year.' And I'd say, 'You want to be 9-7 your whole life? Not me. We want to win the Super Bowl here.' We had a test of wills. He's a knucklehead. His way was simply not going to be good enough."

At that point, King said that Favre was not as confident as he once was. Packers quarterbacks coach Steve Mariucci also tried to get into Favre's head. The former told the young quarterback he had two choices. He could feel sorry for himself, or he could play the best football of his life.

Mariucci's words hit home for Favre. All of a sudden, the football gods flipped a switch. Favre promised "the second half of the season is going to be like no other," per King.

Beginning with a Week 9 encounter against the NFC Central rivals Chicago Bears on the road, the Green Bay Packers won three in a row. They lost their next three games before rallying to win their last three. They went 6-3 during a nine-game span to lock up a second consecutive postseason appearance. Green Bay earned the fourth seed in the NFC.

Brett Favre was spectacular. He reeled off 24 touchdown passes and just seven interceptions after he made his promise to Packers brass. He recorded 3,882 passing yards on the year for good measure.[xxvii] It was enough to place him second in the entire league in that category. One of Favre's best games came against the Tampa Bay Buccaneers on December 24. He completed 24 of 36 pass attempts for 291 yards, three touchdowns, and one interception in a 34-19 win on the road to secure a spot in the playoffs. Favre threw two of his touchdown strikes to wide receiver Sterling Sharpe in the second quarter. Green Bay led at the half, 28-6, and never looked back. It was also Sharpe's last football game – he underwent off-season neck surgery and decided to retire to start a sports broadcasting career.[xxviii]

Next up for the Packers was a rematch against the Detroit Lions in the Wild Card Round. Last season, the Lions had home-field advantage. Now Green Bay had that privilege and Detroit had the lower seed (fifth). Even if the Lions did not enjoy the support of their home crowd, they were out for revenge. They still remembered how Brett Favre had ended their 1993 NFL season with his last-minute touchdown pass a year earlier.

The 1994 NFC Wild Card Game pitting the two squads took place at Lambeau Field on December 31, 1994. Favre and Co.

wanted nothing less than a victory to usher in the New Year. The Packers quarterback, the second-most prolific passer in the 1994 NFL season, failed to record a touchdown pass against the Lions. He did convert 23 of 38 pass attempts for 262 yards and no picks, per PackersHistory.net. Green Bay relied on a rookie Dorsey Levens' three-yard touchdown run in the first quarter and three field goals from Chris Jacke in this game. The Packers' 16 points were enough to beat the Lions, who mustered only 12. Green Bay held Detroit superstar running back Barry Sanders – the league's leading rusher with 1,883 yards – to 1-yard rushing in the worst performance of his career. The Packers also eked out the narrow win without Sharpe, who cheered his former teammates on from the sidelines. Brett Favre also upped his playoff record against the Detroit Lions to 2-0. The Lions had to wait before they got their revenge.

Green Bay next took on the Dallas Cowboys in the 1994 NFC Divisional Round. The Packers' playoff journey in 1994 was the same as the season before when they had faced Detroit and Dallas. The Cowboys controlled the game from start to finish in their 1993 duel against Green Bay. Would it be the same storyline in 1994?

Yes, it was. Dallas scored four touchdowns in the first half. Each of these was from four different players: Emmitt Smith,

Alvin Harper, Blair Thomas, and Scott Galbraith. The Cowboys led at halftime, 28-9. All the Packers could come up with were a Chris Jacke field goal and Edgar Bennet touchdown run (Jacke missed the extra point). They failed to score a point in the second half while allowing another Cowboys touchdown. Final score: Cowboys 35, Packers 9. Brett Favre also did not register a touchdown pass in this game or the entire 1994 postseason, for that matter.

The Green Bay Packers thought they could make strides from their 1993 season. Instead, they ran into a dominant Dallas Cowboys team. Until they beat the Cowboys, they didn't deserve to be considered Super Bowl contenders. Brett Favre's performance suffered when he faced Troy Aikman and Co. for the second straight year. To make matters worse, his contract with the Packers expired. It was an easy call for Packers general manager Ron Wolf. He re-signed his prized recruit to a five-year, $19 million deal.

Now that a new contract was in place, Brett Lorenzo Favre was in a position to avenge the Packers' losses to the Cowboys in the postseason.

1995 NFL Season

Even though Brett Favre had led the Green Bay Packers to a second straight postseason berth, their season had ended prematurely at the hands of the Dallas Cowboys. If Favre and his teammates had one team they needed to beat to make a resounding statement, it was Dallas. Could the two teams be on another collision course in 1995?

If Favre was impressive in 1994, he was even better in 1995. The most glaring difference was his confidence – he had a newfound swagger right from the beginning. He never had to go through the first-half season slump he had to endure in 1994. He didn't have to throw seven interceptions in the team's first seven games so he could turn things around. The Brett Favre of 1995 was a far cry from the one who played with reckless abandon in seasons past.

Behind his leadership, the Packers went 5-2 in their first seven games of the 1995 NFL season. He threw 16 touchdown passes and just six picks during that span. When he played well, so did the Green Bay Packers.

Favre's best game in the first half of the season was in a 38-21 win over their division rivals, the Minnesota Vikings, on October 22, 1995. Favre carved Minnesota's defense for 295 yards, four touchdowns, and no interceptions. After the Packers had lost to the Detroit Lions and Minnesota Vikings, they went on a tear, winning six of their last seven games of the season to finish 11-5 and win the NFC Central Division. It was Green Bay's first division championship with Favre as their starting quarterback. As sweet as it was, it was not the Packers' goal. It was Super Bowl or bust. They earned the NFC's No. 3 seed and home-field advantage in the Wild Card Round.

Favre wound up with the best statistical season of his five-year pro career: 4,413 passing yards, 38 touchdowns, and 13 interceptions.[xxix] His 38 touchdown passes led the NFL. He also piled up on the accolades, securing his third Pro Bowl berth and earned First-Team All-Pro and NFC Player of the Year distinctions as well. To top everything off, the league named Brett Lorenzo Favre the 1995 Most Valuable Player. He had come a long way. Packers general manager Ron Wolf's intuition was right all along: Brett Favre was MVP material.

The upcoming postseason was Favre's chance to prove he was a bona fide MVP to his naysayers. He wanted to put his past playoff failures behind him.

The Green Bay Packers took on the Atlanta Falcons in the 1995 Wild Card Game on December 31, 1995. Once again, the Pack wanted a playoff win to welcome the New Year. For Brett Favre, it was a chance at retribution – he wanted to show the Falcons they had made a mistake in taking his talents for granted. Remember, Atlanta made him the 33rd overall pick in 1991. Favre had a season to forget in Georgia. Since then, he had come a long way in snowy Green Bay, Wisconsin.

The Packers got off to a hot start against the Falcons. Atlanta got on the board first when quarterback Jeff George threw a 65-yard touchdown pass to Eric Metcalf for a 7-0 lead after the point after touchdown (PAT). Edgar Bennett countered with an eight-yard touchdown run. Favre then connected with wide receiver Robert Brooks for a 14-yard score to put Green Bay ahead, 14-7. Falcons kicker Morten Andresen then made a field goal to narrow the gap to four. The Packers seized control with a spectacular 76-yard punt return for a touchdown by Antonio Freeman and another Favre touchdown pass. The Green Bay quarterback found tight end Mark Chmura in the end zone just before halftime to make it 27-10 in the home team's favor.[xxx]

Both teams scored 10 points in the second half to finish off the scoring. Favre's third and last touchdown pass to running back Dorsey Levens in the fourth quarter sealed the deal. The Packers had beaten the Falcons, 37-20. Brett Favre had made a resounding statement to the Falcons. He completed 24 of 35 pass attempts for 199 yards, three touchdowns, and no interceptions.

Green Bay faced a tough test in the 1995 NFC Divisional Round: The No. 2-seeded San Francisco 49ers. Favre squared off against Steve Young and Jerry Rice for the first time in the postseason. Beating those two future Hall of Famers would make it a very sweet victory.

Getting off to a fast start was the key for Green Bay. The last thing the Packers wanted was the 49ers' high-octane offense dictating the tempo in the early going. The Packers met their objective when they scored 21 points in the first half while limiting San Francisco to a solitary field goal. Their defense was solid. Green Bay linebacker Wayne Simmons' hard tackle on San Francisco running back Adam Walker resulted in a fumble in the first quarter. Cornerback Craig Newsome scooped up the football and returned it 31 yards for a touchdown. Favre added two touchdown passes to his tight ends Keith Jackson and Mark Chmura for a commanding halftime lead. Even though the 49ers outscored the Packers 14-6 in the second half, it was not enough. The visitors were moving on. Favre completed 21 of 28 pass attempts for 299 yards, two touchdowns, and no interceptions, per PackersHistory.net. He was about to experience playing in the NFC Championship Game for the first time.

Waiting for the Packers were – who else – the top-seeded Dallas Cowboys. Brett Favre and Co. had lost to this team in the playoffs for two consecutive years. Would they finally be able to end the curse?

This Packers vs. Cowboys tussle was a different one than in recent years past. Dallas would typically establish an early and insurmountable lead and never look back. The 1995 NFC Championship Game was an exciting one from start to finish.

The Packers came back from an early 14-3 first-quarter deficit when Favre threw two touchdown passes to Robert Brooks and Keith Jackson. The former was a 73-yard bomb with two minutes left in the first quarter. The latter was a 24-yard strike with barely a minute gone by in the second quarter. A Chris Boniol field goal and an Emmitt Smith touchdown put the Cowboys up at the half, 24-17. It wouldn't be the last time Smith would hurt the Packers in this contest.

After Chris Jacke had converted on his second field goal, Favre found Brooks in the end zone for the second time. The Packers quarterback connected on a one-yard strike to his wide receiver in the Dallas red zone. Green Bay's defense also held the

Cowboys to a scoreless third quarter. At the end of 45 minutes, the Packers held a 27-24 lead. All they had to do was win the fourth quarter, and they would move on to Super Bowl XXX.

Alas, Emmitt Smith thwarted the Pack's hopes of advancing. First, he scored on a five-yard run to put Dallas up, 31-27. Several plays later, Favre threw his second interception of the game – this time to Cowboys cornerback Larry Brown. Smith made the Packers pay and scored another touchdown to put the game away. Final score: Cowboys 38, Packers 27.

Despite the heartbreaking loss (a third consecutive in the postseason to Dallas), Brett Lorenzo Favre took his playoff performance to a whole new level. He finished the game with 307 yards, three touchdowns, and two interceptions, per PackersHistory.net. The 1995 NFL MVP had made strides, and so did his Packers. If this trend kept up, they could wind up in the Super Bowl the following year.

1996 NFL Season

The Green Bay Packers had won 37 regular-season games in the past four season with Brett Lorenzo Favre as their starting quarterback. It meant they averaged nine wins per year with him under center. He was now a six-year veteran and the 1995 NFL

MVP. With more experience under Favre's belt, he was poised to lead his team to Super Bowl XXXI.

The 1996 NFL season proved beyond doubt the Green Bay Packers were for real. They were juggernauts all season long. Green Bay won six of their first seven games heading into their bye week. The Pack rolled over the opposition by an average of 24 points. Favre was terrific – he recorded 21 touchdown passes and a mere five interceptions. He may have just been 26 years old, but he was already wise beyond his years.

A game which epitomized this was Favre's four-touchdown performance against the Seattle Seahawks on September 29, 1996. It represented a career high for him. He also had no interceptions. In contrast, Seattle quarterback Rick Mirer had his worst game of the season – he threw four interceptions in the Packers' 31-10 win which upped their record to 4-1. According to PackersHistory.net, most of the sellout crowd of 59,973 at the Kingdome in Seattle were Packers fans.[xxxi] Green Bay, Wisconsin was a long way off from the Pacific Northwest. It proved to the entire league how popular Brett Favre and the Packers had become over the years. Call it a throwback to his Southern Miss days when he had a cheering section in every home game. The game against the Seahawks was not a home game, but it felt like one.

Green Bay didn't have much trouble running over its opponents the rest of the way. Favre continued his MVP-caliber performance with 18 touchdowns and just eight interceptions in the second half of the 1996 NFL season. He ran up his total to a league-leading 39 touchdowns and 13 picks for the year.[xxxii] The Packers' remaining nine games were mainly target practice for Favre. Most of their opponents – the Tampa Bay Buccaneers, Detroit Lions, St. Louis Rams (now the Los Angeles Rams), and Chicago Bears – had sub-par seasons. To Green Bay's credit, it beat powerhouses such as the Dallas Cowboys and Denver Broncos. The Packers and the Broncos wound up with the league's best record of 13-3. Green Bay's resounding 41-6 rout of Denver on December 8 served notice Favre and Co. was for real. They won the NFC Central division for a second straight year and received a first-round bye because of their stellar record.

The Packers quarterback earned his fourth Pro Bowl and second First Team All-Pro nods. Favre's dominant performance resulted in his second consecutive NFC Player of the Year and NFL MVP Award.

With an extra week to rest and prepare, the Green Bay Packers were set to take on the San Francisco 49ers in the 1996 NFC Divisional Round. The 49ers had earlier shut out the fifth-seeded Philadelphia Eagles in the NFC Wild Card Game at 3Com Park on December 29, 14-0. It would be Brett Favre vs. Steve Young and Jerry Rice again.

Just like in the previous season's NFC Championship Game, the Packers would jump on the 49ers in the first 30 minutes of play. Green Bay led San Francisco at the half, 21-7. The Packers' Desmond Howard started the game off in electrifying fashion by scoring on a 71-yard punt return for a touchdown to put his team on the board. Green Bay's special teams rose to the occasion again six minutes later after Howard returned the 49ers' Tommy Thompson's punt 46 yards to San Francisco's four-yard line. It set up Favre's four-yard touchdown pass to wide receiver Andre Rison to make it 14-0. Green Bay running back Edgar Bennett continued to perform well in the postseason. His two-yard scamper three minutes later made it 21-0. 49ers quarterback Elvis Grbac threw for a touchdown and ran for another in the second and third quarters. San Francisco trimmed the deficit to just seven, 21-14. Midway through the third quarter, Bennett fumbled in the end zone. However, wide receiver Antonio Freeman recovered the football to make it 28-14. Favre then orchestrated a late six-play drive which culminated in Freeman's 11-yard touchdown for the final score of 35-14. Favre's final stat line was a modest 11-of-15 passing for 79 yards and one touchdown. It was far from his best playoff performance. Green Bay's special teams and running game made the difference in this one. The Pack moved on to the 1996 NFC Championship Game to face the upstart Carolina Panthers.

The Panthers were only in their second year of existence in the National Football League. After a respectable 7-9 mark in their first season, they racked up five more wins in 1996. At 12-4, Carolina had the league's second-best record behind Green Bay and Denver. Players such as quarterback Kerry Collins, running back Anthony Johnson, wide receiver Willie Green, and tight end Wesley Walls carried the load for the Panthers. Could these no-name players possibly upset Brett Favre's Packers?

Nope. Green Bay had too much experience. Losing to the Carolina Panthers in the 1996 NFC Championship Game was not an option. The contest took place at Lambeau Field on January 12, 1997. The first half was a relatively close one with the Packers holding on to a 17-10 advantage. The Panthers stunned them with a three-yard touchdown reception by fullback Howard Griffith to make it 7-0. Touchdowns by running back Dorsey Levens and wide receiver Antonio Freeman helped Green Bay regain control.

The Packers tightened their defense in the second half. After the two squads had traded field goals, Favre engineered a three-play, 74-yard drive which ended with an Edgar Bennett touchdown late in the third quarter. Packers kicker Chris Jacke scored on the insurance field goal early in the fourth quarter to close things off. Final score: Packers 30, Panthers 13. Favre converted on 19 of 29 passes for 292 yards, two touchdowns, and an interception, per PackersHistory.net. Green Bay was moving on to face the New England Patriots in Super Bowl XXXI. It was the Packers' first Super Bowl game since the 1967 NFL season. That season, they beat the Oakland Raiders, 33-14, in Super Bowl II. Green Bay's legendary head coach Vince Lombardi won his second straight league title. It took the Packers 29 long years before they could reach the Super Bowl again. With Brett Favre at the helm, they had a good chance to win their third title since the historic AFL-NFL merger in 1966.

Super Bowl XXXI

It took Brett Lorenzo Favre six years to reach the Super Bowl. His NFL career got off to a rough start with the Atlanta Falcons. He was fortunate that Green Bay Packers general manager Ron Wolf never stopped pursuing him. In 1992, Cheeseheads had no idea who Brett Favre was or what he was capable of doing. Fast forward several years later, he became a two-time NFL MVP and league passing leader who could finally help them win the Vince Lombardi Trophy after an agonizing 29-year wait.

The final hurdles Favre and the Packers had to clear were Bill Parcells and the New England Patriots.

Super Bowl XXXI took place at the Louisiana Superdome in New Orleans on February 3, 1997. New Orleans is just an hour's drive away from Favre's hometown of Kiln, Miss. Needless to say, he had a large cheering section once again. That's Brett Favre for you – a great football player with an entertaining personality. A lot of people like him.

Unfortunately for Favre, the road to the Super Bowl wasn't going to be easy for him.

According *to Sports Illustrated's* Michael Silver, Favre came down with a 101-degree flu the Thursday before the big game. He stayed in his hotel room shivering under his comforter.

"I was worried," Favre told Silver. "I'd waited my whole life to play in this game, and now I wasn't going to be healthy. But the night before the game I slept great. I fell asleep at 9:30 with the TV clicker in my hand, and I felt pretty good when I woke up. But I was nervous before kickoff, and I kept dry-heaving all game."[xxxiii]

Apparently, the after effects of Favre's bug barely sidetracked him in Super Bowl XXXI. On the Packers' second play from scrimmage, he threw a 54-yard touchdown pass to wide receiver Andre Rison on a wide post pattern. Green Bay cornerback Doug Evans intercepted New England quarterback Drew Bledsoe on the ensuing series. It results in a Chris Jacke 37-yard field goal for a 10-0 Packers lead.

Bledsoe shook off the sting of his interception to throw two touchdown passes in the first quarter alone – one to fullback Keith Byars and the other to tight end Ben Coates. New England led for the first time, 14-10. It was the highest-scoring first quarter in Super Bowl history, (tied with six other games, the most recent being Super Bowl XLV between the Green Bay Packers and Pittsburgh Steelers, per NFL.com)[xxxiv]. Despite Bledsoe's heroics, he would finish the game with four picks.

Favre countered with an 81-yard touchdown strike to wide receiver Antonio Freeman. Favre saw Patriots strong safety Lawyer Milloy at the line of scrimmage. He had been waiting to cover Freeman. The Packers quarterback lofted a beautiful aerial to Freeman to make it 17-14 for Green Bay. Jacke scored a field goal, and Favre ran the ball into the end zone in the waning moments of the second quarter to increase their lead to 27-14 at the half. The Patriots threatened in the third quarter when running back Curtis Martin scored on an 18-yard run to trim the deficit to just six.

And then the backbreaker occurred.

Packers punt returner Desmond Howard, who accepted a near-minimum $300,000 salary for the 1996 NFL season, told Favre at halftime, "I'm going to take one of those kicks back; it's only a matter of time."

His prophecy became a reality with just over three minutes remaining in the third quarter. He caught the ball at the one-yard line, turned on the afterburners, and left the entire New England special teams players biting his dust. Touchdown. Without a doubt, his 99-yard kickoff return for a score was the most spectacular play in the game. It came as no surprise he won Super Bowl XXXI MVP honors.

After Howard's scintillating play, the score was 35-21 for Green Bay. Neither team scored in the fourth quarter. The Green Bay Packers had won their 12th NFL championship and third Super Bowl title. The once bed-ridden Favre completed 14 of 27 passes for 246 yards and two touchdowns, per PackersHistory.net. He and his teammates had done it. They were world champions. Favre – who had amassed all sorts of accolades in recent years – finally won the one that mattered the most.

It was a bittersweet moment for him. He had lost his best friend, Mark Haverty, who died in a car accident in the offseason (Favre's brother Scott was the driver).

"Through everything," Favre told Silver after the game. "I really believed I'd be here today. Right here in this stairwell, talking about being world champions. My best friend's gone forever. Trouble never seems to be far away, and the future won't be all rosy, but they can't take this away from me. Thirty years from now, the kids will be getting ready for Super Bowl LXI, and NFL Films will drag out Steve Sabol – he'll be around 102 then – and he'll talk about how Brett Favre fought through such adversity. And there will be other players and coaches. But I know this: We etched our place in history today."

Brett Favre could not have said it any better.

1997 NFL Season

The 1997 NFL offseason was Brett Favre's most memorable to date. He and his Green Bay Packers had won Super Bowl XXXI. They spent the next several months resting their bodies and basking in the glory of their historic achievement. As the new season grew nearer, they set their minds on a new goal: winning another one. Everybody in the National Football League would be after them. They now had a bulls-eye on their backs. If it were up to them, they would rather be known as the standard of excellence in professional football.

This season was a virtual repeat of the previous one – the Packers found ways to win. And they didn't just win, they did it consistently.

Green Bay won five of their first seven games in 1997. They beat playoff contenders such as the Miami Dolphins, Minnesota Vikings, and Tampa Bay Buccaneers along the way. In that particular seven-game stretch, Brett Favre threw for 15 touchdowns and eight interceptions.

His best game early on was the one against the Vikings. Even though he threw two picks, he also had five touchdown passes. He connected with four different receivers: Robert Brooks, Antonio Freeman, Terry Mickens, and Mark Chmura. The fact that Favre had a broad array of weapons at his disposal proved how deadly Green Bay's offense was. The Packers overcame Vikings running back Robert Smith's 132 yards to prevail, 38-32. It was the former's 21st consecutive victory at Lambeau Field.[xxxv]

Green Bay was virtually unbeatable after their bye week, winning eight of their last nine games. Ironically, the lone setback came at the hands of the 3-13 Indianapolis Colts on November 16. The Colts, the league's worst team, squeaked by the Packers with a 41-38 win. Cary Blanchard's field goal with no time left gave Indy its first win of the season (and at the expense of the defending Super Bowl champions at that). Brett Favre finished with 18-of-25 passing for 363 yards, three touchdowns, and two interceptions, per PackersHistory.net.

A week later, Favre and Co. bounced back with an emphatic 45-17 win over the once-mighty Dallas Cowboys, who had fallen on hard times. The Cowboys finished the 1997 NFL season with a 6-10 record and missed the postseason for the first time in seven years. Favre was at his best against Dallas with 203 passing yards, four touchdowns, and just one interception. Green Bay won their next four games to run their season-ending winning streak to five. The Pack wound up with another stellar 13-3 record. They were NFC Central champions yet again, earning the conference's No. 2 seed (behind the 13-3 San Francisco 49ers) and a bye in the NFC Wild Card Round.

Favre concluded the 1997 regular season with 3,867 passing yards, 35 touchdowns, and 16 interceptions. The awards continued to pour on. He earned his fifth Pro Bowl nod, third straight First Team All-Pro selection, third consecutive NFC Player of the Year Award, and third straight NFL MVP Award. That early, the 28-year-old signal caller had "Pro Football Hall of Fame" written all over him.

Favre may have had another season for the ages, but it was time to get down to more serious business: Defending their Super Bowl title.

First up was Trent Dilfer and the Tampa Bay Buccaneers, who beat the Detroit Lions, 20-10, in the 1997 NFC Wild Card Round. The 1997 NFC Divisional Round game – the first one between the two squads in the postseason – took place at Lambeau Field on January 4, 1998. It was a tough, grind-it-out affair. Favre threw a three-yard touchdown pass to tight end Mark Chmura with 5:36 remaining in the first quarter. Packers kicker Ryan Longwell scored two field goals in the second quarter to pad the lead even further. The Bucs failed to score in the first half – a testament to the Packers' tight defense. Green Bay led after the first 30 minutes, 13-0.

The Packers were in a position to put the game out of reach when Antonio Freeman returned the second half's opening kickoff 90 yards. However, the officials called Green Bay safety Darren Sharper for a 10-yard holding penalty and nullified

Freeman's kickoff return. Favre remained undaunted. He helped the Packers moved the sticks to Tampa Bay's 25-yard line. However, they could go no further after Buccaneers cornerback Donnie Abraham swatted Favre's pass on fourth down, forcing the home team to punt. Tampa Bay went on a 94-yard scoring drive which ended in a Mike Alstott touchdown – their only one in the game. Packers running back Dorsey Levens then scored a goal with 13:37 remaining in the contest. Favre converted the two-point conversion on a quarterback draw for the final score of 21-7. He teased the Lambeau Field crowd by trying to dunk the football over the crossbar. For the game, he converted on 15 of 28 pass attempts for 190 yards, one touchdown, and two interceptions.

The Packers next took on a familiar opponent in the 1997 NFC Championship Game: The San Francisco 49ers.

Favre admitted to *Sports Illustrated's* Michael Silver he was very nervous before the game. The reason? He was about to go up against his former quarterback coach and mentor, Steve Mariucci. The 49ers had hired him to be their head coach before the 1997 NFL season.

"I was real nervous last night," Favre told Silver. "I said more prayers before this game than before any game I ever remember.

No formal prayers, but just praying for, well, wisdom, I guess. We were playing a great team with a great defense, and I just prayed that I'd play smart and make good decisions."[xxxvi]

According to Silver, Packers head coach Mike Holmgren tweaked his game plan for the 49ers. Instead of resorting to a maximum of eight passes for every 15 plays Green Bay ran, Holmgren wanted his men to pass nine times. Favre remembered it being the most his head coach allowed in his six years in Packers Green and Gold. Passing nine times allowed him to test the mettle of the San Francisco secondary, which had the likes of Rod Woodson and Marquez Pope.

It turned out that the new strategy threw the 49ers off. They managed just three points in the first half while allowing their opponents to score 13. Longwell started things off with a field goal in the waning moments of the first quarter. San Francisco had a golden opportunity to pull ahead when quarterback Steve Young orchestrated a key drive punctuated by a 43-yard throw to wide receiver J.J. Stokes. It moved the sticks to the Green Bay 30-yard line. Three plays later, on 3rd and 8, Young tried to throw the ball to tight end Brent Jones. However, Packers free safety Eugene Robinson stepped into the passing lane and picked Young off. Robinson took the ball all the way to San Francisco's 28-yard line. On second down, the Brett Favre-

Antonio Freeman connection struck. Freeman's 27-yard reception made it 10-0. The 49ers' Gary Anderson and the Packers' Ryan Longwell then traded field goals in the second quarter.

Longwell added another field goal in the third quarter. Running back Dorsey Levens then scored on a five-yard touchdown run with 3:10 left to play. The San Francisco 49ers were done. The Cheeseheads that were on hand at 3Com Park erupted in celebration. Even Chuck Levy's 95-yard kickoff return for a touchdown 18 seconds later couldn't put a damper on the festivities, even if Green Bay was more than two thousand miles away.

Brett Favre had another respectable playoff performance: 16-of-27 passing for 222 yards, one touchdown, and no interception. It was a good showing considering the soggy field conditions. The San Francisco defense also managed to sack him just once. Favre's counterpart, Steve Young, threw for 250 yards, no touchdowns, and one interception. The Green Bay defense swarmed him all day long, sacking him four times for a net loss of 26 yards, per PackersHistory.net.

The Green Bay Packers were now in the Super Bowl for the second consecutive year. Remember, they had not won the

Vince Lombardi Trophy since 1967 before their Super Bowl XXX conquest of the New England Patriots. Winning consecutive Super Bowl titles would be the ultimate vindication for the franchise.

The team which stood in Green Bay's way was the Denver Broncos. Their quarterback was John Elway, another future Hall of Famer who wanted nothing more than a win in the season finale. Elway made headlines when he refused to play for the then-Baltimore Colts – one of the league's worst teams – after they drafted him first overall in 1983. He did not soften his stance one bit. To the Colts' dismay, they were forced to trade him to the Denver Broncos for offensive lineman Chris Hinton. The rest, as they say, is history.

Denver had missed the postseason for three straight years before acquiring Elway from Baltimore. Once he got on board, the helped turned the Broncos into contenders – they played in three Super Bowl games in the 1980s, but unfortunately lost them all. In the 1997 NFL season, Elway was already a battle-tested 15-year veteran who ached for a Super Bowl ring. Brett Favre and the Green Bay Packers had other plans. It was destined to be a tremendous matchup.

Super Bowl XXXII took place at Qualcomm Stadium in San Diego, California on January 25, 1998, before a capacity crowd of 68,912. It was a close game throughout. The Packers drew first blood after they marched 76 yards downfield in just four minutes. Favre threw a 22-yard touchdown strike to Antonio Freeman to open up the scoring. Elway and Co. marched 58 yards down the field in the ensuing series. Denver running back Terrell Davis' one-yard plunge tied the score at seven apiece.

The next few plays were something Brett Favre wanted to forget. He first threw an interception to Broncos safety, Tyrone Braxton. It resulted in Elway rushing in for a touchdown on 3rd-and-goal. On Green Bay's ensuing series, Denver safety Steve Atwater forced Favre to fumble. The Broncos recovered at their opponents' 33-yard line. Denver kicker Jason Elam made a 51-yard field goal moments later to make it 17-7 for his team. Favre made up for his miscues by throwing a six-yard touchdown pass to tight end Mark Chmura to inch within three points at the half.

Davis fumbled on Denver's first play from scrimmage in the second half. The Packers' Ryan Longwell converted a field goal to tie the game at 17. Both teams went three-and-out in the next two series. Elway's 36-yard pass to Ed McCaffrey was the highlight of a crucial 92-yard drive which culminated in Davis' second touchdown of the game. Freeman fumbled at the Packers' 22-yard line early in the fourth quarter. Elway had a golden opportunity to put the Pack away, but Green Bay free safety Eugene Robinson intercepted his pass in the end zone on the ensuing possession. Freeman caught a touchdown pass from Favre with 13:32 left in the game to tie things up again. The Packers then committed two very costly penalties which put the Broncos in a position to score in the next series. Davis scored on a one-yard touchdown run with 1:45 remaining. Favre managed to lead Green Bay to Denver's 35-yard line, but they could not get any closer to the end zone. Broncos linebacker John Mobley batted down Favre's desperation pass to tight end Mark Chmura on fourth down to secure Denver's first Super Bowl title. Final Score: Denver 31, Green Bay 24. The Broncos' win snapped a 13-game winning streak for the NFC in the Super Bowl.

Favre connected on 25 of 42 passes for 256 yards, three touchdowns, and one interception, per PackersHistory.net. Davis – who scored three goals – ran away with Super Bowl XXXII MVP honors.

The Green Bay Packers did not achieve their goal of winning consecutive Super Bowl titles. Even if that were the case, they gave it all they had. They had just lost to a better and hungrier team. The good news was that the Packers were far from done – they were still out to compete for another title in 1998.

1998 NFL Season

After losing to the Denver Broncos in Super Bowl XXXII, the Green Bay Packers had to prove to everyone that they were capable of bouncing back. They had three-time NFL MVP Brett Favre leading the charge. He was barely 29 years old heading into the 1998 NFL season. At that age, a quarterback was just approaching his prime. Favre had a lot of good years left.

The Packers started the season off on a four-game winning streak. They beat the Detroit Lions, Tampa Bay Buccaneers, Cincinnati Bengals, and Carolina Panthers by an average of 10 points. Favre had ten touchdown passes and four interceptions during the streak. He threw for a season-high five touchdown passes to go along with three picks in the 37-30 road win over the Panthers on September 27, 1998. Third-year wide receiver Derrick Mayes hauled in three touchdown receptions in the victory. The Packers also amassed a season-high 487 yards while limiting the Panthers to just 230 yards. Green Bay defensive ends Reggie White and Vonnie Holliday both made life miserable for Carolina quarterback Kerry Collins – they each sacked him twice. It was a great victory on both sides of the ball for the Packers.[xxxvii]

The law of averages then caught up with Favre and Co. – they lost their next two games to the Minnesota Vikings and Detroit Lions. Favre was inefficient, throwing for just two touchdowns and six interceptions in those two contests. The Vikings even held him to a season-low 114 yards and no touchdown passes in their 37-24 win over the Packers on October 5, 1998, per PackersHistory.net. Favre was only human after all. Even a three-time NFL MVP can have his off-days.

Despite Favre's sub-par performance in Minnesota, the Packers regrouped and won seven of their final ten games. He turned in a so-so performance the rest of the way with 19 touchdown passes and 13 interceptions.[xxxviii] Favre's performance regressed because of two things. First, opposing defenses did a better job of scouting him. They were able to stymie him with blitzes and other strategies which forced him to throw errant passes. Secondly, his age might have caught up with him. He wasn't even 30 years old yet, but with linebackers pounding his body week after week, he could have been ten years older. Imagine agile, 250-lb. men coming at you full throttle for 16 weeks in the regular season. Brett Favre had apparently hit a wall in his eighth pro season. He had to shake off its effects by the time the postseason began.

Favre's best game before the playoffs was a 30-22 road win over the Tennessee Oilers (now the Tennessee Titans) on December 20, 1998. He recorded 253 passing yards, three touchdown passes, and no interceptions in that game, per NFL.com. His sidekick, wide receiver Antonio Freeman, was just as spectacular with 186 receiving yards and three touchdowns. According to PackersHistory.net, Favre upped his season touchdown pass total to 30. It marked the fifth straight year with at least 30 touchdown strikes.

Favre wound up with 4,212 passing yards, 31 touchdown passes, and 23 interceptions (the most since his third year in the NFL, when he had 24 interceptions). Because his performance dipped, his three-year reign as NFL MVP had ended. He also didn't make it to the Pro Bowl for the first time in four years. The 1998 NFL season was a tough one for Brett Lorenzo Favre, and it was about to get tougher.

The Green Bay Packers finished with an 11-5 record, which was good enough for second in the NFC Central division. The Minnesota Vikings ran away with the division championship due to their spectacular 15-1 record. As for the Packers, they got the fifth seed in the NFC and a date with their familiar foes – the fourth-seeded San Francisco 49ers – in the Wild Card Round.

Their playoff game commenced on January 3, 1999, at San Francisco's 3Com Park. The breaks just didn't go Green Bay's way in the end game. On this day, the 49ers' running game proved to be unstoppable – they amassed 178 yards on the ground. Running back Garrison Hearst rushed for 128 yards, per *The Milwaukee Journal Sentinel's* Bob McGinn.[xxxix] Combine the 49ers' dominant running game with Favre's sub-par performance, and you have a recipe for disaster.

Favre continued to throw the football away at an alarming rate, recording two more untimely interceptions against the 49ers. Not only that, he also fumbled three times. Packers running back Dorsey Levens amassed 153 all-purpose yards to keep his team's hopes alive.

The Packers led, 27-23, with just eight seconds left in the game. McGinn said that the 49ers ran a four-vertical route where four of their receivers ran as fast as they could. San Francisco quarterback Steve Young spotted Terrell Owens as he ran a corner route from the right slot. Packers safety Darren Sharper lost track of Owens as he ran, and the latter was able to catch the football with just three seconds left. Touchdown. Game over. Final Score: San Francisco 30, Green Bay 27.

It was also Mike Holmgren's last game as Packers head coach.

Five days after the loss to the 49ers, Holmgren accepted the Seattle Seahawks' eight-year head coaching offer valued at more than $4 million annually, per *The Milwaukee Journal Sentinel's* Tom Silverstein. Holmgren also became the Seahawks' executive vice president of football operations.[xl] The Favre-Holmgren relationship had officially ended.

Favre told *The Milwaukee Journal Sentinel's* Lori Nickel on November 12, 2005 – almost seven years after Holmgren left – that he never expected his head coach to leave.

"Everyone talked about him leaving," Favre quipped. "I said, 'You're crazy.' I was so naïve. The year before, at the Super Bowl we lost, that week, all the press conferences, they asked the question to me: What I thought about Mike Holmgren possibly leaving. I thought it was the stupidest question I'd ever heard. First time I'd ever heard it. I thought that question was odd, off the wall, and forgot about it…Well, a year later, he left; and I expected us to be together forever."[xli]

The 1998 NFL season was one Brett Favre would rather forget. After so many rough patches, there was no question he was looking for brighter things in 1999.

1999 NFL Season

Brett Favre had one thing in mind in 1999: Putting the disastrous 1998 season behind him and starting anew with his new head coach, former Philadelphia Eagles mentor Ray Rhodes. The Eagles had steadily regressed under his guidance from 1995-98. They won 10 games in each of his first two seasons before finishing with a 6-10 record in 1997. They reached rock bottom in 1998, winning just three games. The Eagles fired him in December of that year.

Fortunately, Green Bay came calling. The Packers hired him to be their new head coach on January 11, 1999. According to *The Milwaukee Journal Sentinel* (via CBS Sports), they signed him to a four-year deal which paid him roughly $1 million annually.[xlii] Rhodes was former Green Bay head coach Mike Holmgren's defensive coordinator from 1992-93 – Brett Favre's first two years in Packers Green and Gold.

Big questions loomed for the Packers. Would Rhodes be able to resurrect their fading playoff hopes? Would he be able to co-exist with his players, most notably Favre, the three-time NFL MVP?

The answer to the first question became more apparent as the 1999 NFL season wore on: The Packers were not playoff contenders that year. Green Bay started off well. The team won four of their first six games. Favre wasn't the MVP he was from 1995-97, throwing ten touchdown passes and eight interceptions during that six-game span.[xliii]

And then the bottom fell out.

If Favre's nightmarish performance against the Denver Broncos on October 17, 1999, was any indication, the Packers were in for a very long season. He failed to throw a single touchdown pass while recording three interceptions. He threw for just 120 yards in a 31-10 loss on the road, per NFL.com. According to PackersHistory.net, it was "statistically his worst performance as a pro." It also turned out he had been struggling the entire season with a thumb injury.[xliv]

"I didn't expect to play like this," Favre told the website. "I didn't expect to lose like this. Games like this happen. It was ugly. This is a character check. My thumb has been bothering me all year, but it is not an excuse."

It may not have been an excuse, but it was apparent the injured thumb had severely affected Favre's game. The Packers won just four of their next ten games. He had more interceptions than touchdown passes during that span (16 to 14). He finished the year with 4,091 passing yards, 22 touchdowns, and 23 interceptions, per NFL.com. He was nowhere near the MVP he was for three straight seasons. Instead, he played like the 24-year-old version of himself who had thrown 24 interceptions several years earlier. To top it all off, Green Bay was a shade of its old championship version – the team won just eight games in 1999. They finished third in the NFC Central Division behind the Tampa Bay Buccaneers (11-5) and Minnesota Vikings (10-6). Consequently, the Packers missed the postseason for the first time in seven years (the Dallas Cowboys' season-ending 26-18 win over the New York Giants resulted in the former snagging the NFC's final playoff spot). The last time they had missed the playoffs was in 1992 – Brett Favre's first year in Green Bay.

An 8-8 win-loss record may have sat well with some general managers, but not the Packers' Ron Wolf. He fired Rhodes and his entire staff on January 2, 2000. Ironically, Wolf told *The Associated Press* (via PackersHistory.net) that the idea of dismissing Rhodes after just one year was "ludicrous."

A little more than two weeks after Wolf fired Rhodes, he hired former Green Bay Packers assistant and Seattle Seahawks offensive coordinator Mike Sherman on January 18, 2000, per PackersHistory.net. Sherman was a long-time assistant at the collegiate level. Among his stints were at Tulane, Holy Cross, Texas A&M, and UCLA. Despite having just three years of NFL coaching experience, Sherman earned the confidence of the Packers brass. He had a daunting task ahead of him – resurrect the struggling team and their quarterback heading into the new millennium.

2000 NFL Season

The Green Bay Packers were reeling from the sting of an 8-8 season and elimination from playoff contention in the 1999 NFL season. Brett Lorenzo Favre was also on the cusp of turning 31 years old. After suffering through two consecutive sub-par seasons, he had shown his age. He no longer befuddled opposing teams with his passing savvy. They knew how to get the better of him. Favre's injured thumb also contributed to his decline in 1999. An older and injured Brett Favre spelled trouble for the Green Bay Packers. However, they had a new head coach: Mike Sherman. The former Green Bay assistant knew the system. He had to make it work for everybody involved. The Packers had tried to adjust to former head coach Ray Rhodes' system in 1998. General manager Ron Wolf then fired him in January 2000. With a new head coach calling the shots, Green Bay had to adjust all over again.

The Mike Sherman era got off to a rough start: The Packers lost four of their first six games. The tough part was they lost by an average of barely six points per contest. They kept up with the likes of the New York Jets and Detroit Lions, but just could not get it going in the end game. Favre was so-so once again: nine touchdown passes and eight interceptions.[xlv]

The Packers beat the San Francisco 49ers, 31-28, on October 15, 2000. It was a much-needed win heading into their bye week. Favre connected on 20 of 27 passes for 266 yards in the win, per PackersHistory.net. Packers kicker Ryan Longwell saved the day for his team by nailing the game-winning 35-yarder with just 54 seconds left.

The Packers went through a topsy-turvy month of November. They alternated wins and losses, going 2-3 during that month. Favre was average, throwing for five touchdowns and five interceptions, per NFL.com. Tampa Bay Buccaneers defensive lineman Warren Sapp sacked Favre in the third quarter of the Bucs' 20-15 victory over the Pack on November 12. Favre's foot got wedged underneath the 303-lb. Sapp's body. The Packers quarterback did not return to the game. He finished with 14-of-25 passing for 117 yards. His backup, Matt Hasselbeck, threw for 93 yards and a touchdown in his absence, per PackersHistory.net.[xlvi] At the end of November, the Packers were a below average football club. They had a 5-7 win-loss record and were in danger of missing the postseason for the second year in a row.

The defining moment for Favre and Co. was the month of December. They won all four of their games to finish the 2000 NFL season with a 9-7 win-loss record. They beat the opposition by an average of almost 11 points per game. They also beat division rivals and playoff contenders the Minnesota Vikings and Tampa Bay Buccaneers along the way. The 31-year-old Favre had five touchdown passes and three interceptions in December.

However, it was not enough. Green Bay missed the playoffs yet again. Despite improving their record, the Packers were going home for the offseason. Had they won at least ten games, they would have been in contention for a playoff spot. They faltered early and had to dig themselves out of a hole.

Brett Favre concluded the 2000 NFL season with 20 touchdown passes and 16 interceptions. It was the first time he threw fewer than 23 interceptions in three seasons. Nonetheless, he was far from the NFL MVP he was three years earlier. Age and injuries had crept up on the gunslinger from Kiln, Mississippi. He had to prove the naysayers wrong and get a second lease on life once the 2001 NFL season commenced.

2001 NFL Season

Two significant events occurred as the Green Bay Packers ushered in the new millennium.

First, Brett Favre – the embattled three-time MVP who had struggled in the past three seasons – signed a lucrative deal on March 2, 2001. According to *The Milwaukee Journal Sentinel's* Tom Silverstein, Favre signed a 10-year contract "worth as much as $100 million." He also earned a signing bonus between $10 million and $15 million. He had three years remaining on the seven-year, $47.25 million contract he signed in July 1997. The new mega deal set the 31-year-old Favre for life.[xlvii] It was a clear sign that the Packers still trusted him despite his age, struggles, and injuries.

"I enjoy it here," Favre told Silverstein and other reporters during a conference call. "I don't want to move. I enjoy the fans.

I just want to stay. I couldn't envision myself playing for another team. If that would ever come up, I'd probably just retire. I'd made enough money that I don't need to jump ship and go somewhere else. So it was just important to me to stay here."

Second, Packers executive vice president and general manager Ron Wolf – the man who had brought Brett Favre to Green Bay in 1992 – announced he would retire on June 1, 2001. The team named head coach Mike Sherman to assume Wolf's general manager duties, per Packers.com.[xlviii]

The team enshrined the 62-year-old Wolfe in the Packers Hall of Fame in July 2000. During his eight-year tenure, he guided Green Bay to the NFL's second-best regular-season record. The Packers went 92-52 (.639) under his leadership, per their official website. The team also won Super Bowl XXXI with Wolf as their general manager.

"What people said couldn't happen here," Wolf told Packers.com. "Happened here. I'm proud of that. My goal in coming here was to win 100 games in 10 years. We won 100 games, including the playoffs, in nine years."

In 2001, the Packers' goal was no different. They wanted to re-establish their winning ways. It was Brett Favre's time for redemption.

Brett Favre started off the new millennium on a high note. He threw for 1,568 yards and 14 touchdown passes in the Packers' first six games and managed to limit his interceptions to seven. As a result, Green Bay went 4-2 as it headed into its bye week.[xlix]

Favre's best game in the season's first half was against the Baltimore Ravens on October 14, 2001. He had converted on 27 of 34 passes for 337 yards, three touchdowns, and no interceptions in the hard-earned 31-23 win[l]. Favre turned 32 years old the week before. The victory was a good birthday gift for him.

According to *Sports Illustrated's* Peter King, it was Favre's 150th NFL game. At the time, Favre dubbed it the best game he had ever played, considering the Ravens' ferocious defense. Defensive linemen Sam Adams and Tony Siragusa had helped Baltimore prevent opposing running backs from gaining 100 yards in 38 straight games. Ray Lewis, Michael McCrary, Peter Boulware, Chris McAlister, and Duane Starks were other key components of that defense.[li] Favre got the better of them in Week 5.

"I'm not in fear of anyone," Favre told King. "But I watched six Baltimore games on tape. I saw that so many teams have chances but never capitalize. When (offensive coordinator) Tom Rossley talked to our offense about the game last week, he told us we could have 400 yards if we executed right."

It turned out that Favre fell just 63 yards short of amassing those 400 yards all by himself. He had regained his mojo.

The Packs' good fortunes continued as the 2001 NFL season wore on. After their bye week, they won eight of their last 10 games to finish 12-4, per NFL.com. It was their best record since 1997, the same year Brett Favre signed his seven-year, $47.25 million deal.

The defining moment for Green Bay was on December 23, 2001. On that day, they beat the visiting Cleveland Browns in snowy Lambeau Field, 30-7. They secured a postseason berth for the first time since 1998. Favre completed 18 of 28 passes for 139 yards, three touchdowns, and no interceptions, per *The Associated Press* (via ESPN). He had also set an NFL record by recording his sixth 30-touchdown season. He also upped his record to 29-0 when playing in 34 degrees or colder.[lii] It was quite ironic, as he grew up in the hot and humid Mississippi weather. Green Bay was an excellent fit.

Favre had an excellent bounce-back season. He finished the 2001 NFL season with 3,921 yards, 32 touchdowns, and 15 interceptions, per the league's official website. He also earned a Pro Bowl berth after not making it for the past three seasons. Additionally, the league named him to its Second Team All-Pro lineup for the first time. Brett Favre dealt with adversity for three years. With fierce determination, he was able to overcome the odds. At 32 years of age, he was far from finished.

The Packers secured the NFC's fourth seed and a date in the 2001 NFC Wild Card Game against the San Francisco 49ers on January 13, 2002. It was Green Bay's first home playoff game since 1997.

It was a low-scoring, bruising affair in the first 30 minutes. With barely four minutes to go in the first quarter, Favre found wide receiver Antonio Freeman for a five-yard touchdown. San Francisco defensive lineman Dana Stubblefield blocked Ryan Longwell's extra-point attempt for a 6-0 Packers' lead. The Packers returned the favor after defensive tackle Cletidus Hunt blocked 49ers kicker Jose Cortez's field-goal attempt early in the second quarter. San Francisco quarterback Jeff Garcia helped his team march the football methodically down the field. He led a 15-play, 86-yard drive late in the first half. 49ers running back Garrison Hearst finally put his team on the board with a two-yard touchdown plunge with 11 seconds left in the second quarter, per PackersHistory.net.

After Longwell had converted on a field goal, Favre threw his second touchdown pass of the game when he found tight end Bubba Franks late in the third quarter. It was a 19-yard strike which put the Packers up, 15-7. Donald Driver failed to haul in Favre's two-point conversion pass.

With three minutes gone by in the fourth quarter, the 49ers tied the score after Garcia hit wide receiver Tai Streets in stride for a 14-yard touchdown. San Francisco converted on the two-point conversion to make it 15-all. Longwell regained the lead for Green Bay after he made a 45-yard field goal with seven minutes left to play. The Packers resorted to their running game to put the 49ers away. Ahman Green's nine-yard touchdown run just after the two-minute warning put Green Bay up, 25-15. Green finished with 86 rushing yards on 21 carries, per PackersHistory.net, and the 49ers were unable to narrow the gap. The Packers were moving on to the 2001 NFC Divisional Round. Brett Favre had 269 passing yards, two touchdowns, and one interception.

Next up for Green Bay was the St. Louis Rams. It was another game which Brett Favre would rather forget.

The 2001 NFC Divisional Round took place at the Rams' Edward Jones Dome on January 20, 2002. St. Louis cornerback Aeneas Williams would be the thorn in Favre's side all game long.

Williams picked off Favre at the 9:11 mark of the first quarter. He returned the ball 29 yards for a touchdown to put the Rams up, 7-0. St. Louis quarterback and Super Bowl XXXIV MVP Kurt Warner outplayed Favre in the first half. He threw touchdown passes to Torry Holt and James Hodgins to help the Rams build on their lead. They led at the half, 24-10.

St. Louis poured it on in the second half. Running back Marshall Faulk scored on a seven-yard run and linebacker Tommy Polley tipped a Favre pass intended for running back Ahman Green. Polley took the ball the other way for a touchdown. Williams recorded his second pick-six at Favre's expense midway through the fourth quarter. The game was never close. Although Favre passed for 281 yards and two touchdowns, he also threw a career-high six interceptions in the defeat. According to PackersHistory.net, it was the worst playoff loss in franchise history.

Despite the embarrassing setback, the Packers became contenders again in the 2001 NFL season. They won 12 games under the leadership of a rejuvenated Favre. He just couldn't sustain his momentum in the postseason. Packers fans hoped for a happier ending in 2002.

2002 NFL Season

The Green Bay Packers re-established themselves as title contenders in 2001. It was a long, arduous climb. They were mediocre for three seasons. They had missed the playoffs during that period. They were a team far removed from their glory days when they won Super Bowl XXXI in 1997. Brett Favre was at the center of it all. He had put his bad days behind him. He made a resounding statement in 2001. Would he be able to bring the Pack back to the Promised Land in 2002?

A divisional re-alignment took place in the National Football League that year. The Packers had been part of the NFC Central for quite some time. In 2002, the NFC North division was born. Aside from the Packers, the other teams in this division were the Detroit Lions, Chicago Bears, and Minnesota Vikings.[liii] The re-alignment worked in the Packers' favor. That year, all three of their divisional opponents were not playoff contenders. Six of the Packers' 16 games every year would be against the Lions, Bears, and Vikings. If they swept all six matches, they would have a huge advantage. Green Bay had to be at its best to make sure it locked up the No. 1 seed in the NFC.

The Packers wasted no time in running over the opposition. They went 6-1 in their first seven games, beating their opponents by an average of almost 11 points. Favre was sensational, throwing for 14 touchdowns and just three interceptions.[liv]

One game which stood out was the October 7 encounter against the Chicago Bears at Soldier Field. Favre threw all three of his touchdown passes in a 34-21 pasting of the Packers' division foes. Heading into the game, he needed just 262 yards for a career total of 40,000. He had 359 yards for this contest and achieved his goal of reaching 40,000 yards as early as halftime, when he had already thrown for 287 yards, per *The Associated Press* (via ESPN).[lv]

"I would never in a million years think we'd have a first quarter like we did today, but you never know in this league," he told *The Associated Press*. "This one ranks near the top. You have 300 yards at halftime and three touchdowns, something is working."

Ever since Favre had donned Packers Green and Gold in 1992, he had helped make the rivalry a one-sided one. Green Bay had won 15 of its 17 encounters against Chicago after its most recent victory. More impressively, Favre had led the Packers to nine straight wins over the Bears on the road.

The Packers sported an impressive 8-2 record heading into their Week 12 game against the Tampa Bay Buccaneers, their former division rivals who were now part of the new NFC South. In 2002, former Oakland Raiders head coach Jon Gruden called the shots for the Buccaneers. The latter also had an 8-2 record, the best in the league. Something had to give.

Tampa Bay got the better of Green Bay on this night. Favre had a forgettable game, connecting on 20 of 38 passes for 196 yards, one touchdown, and four interceptions in the 21-7 defeat. He fell to 0-5 all-time at the Buccaneers' Raymond James Stadium.[lvi]

Despite Favre throwing for 34 touchdowns and going 14-6 all-time against Tampa Bay, he had also thrown 19 interceptions against the Bucs. Tampa Bay had the league's stingiest defense. After its conquest of the Packers, the team led the NFL with 25 interceptions, per *The Associated Press.*

After the game, Packers head coach and general manager Mike Sherman had a heated exchange with Buccaneers All-Pro defensive tackle Warren Sapp. Sherman didn't appreciate Sapp's vicious block on Green Bay offensive tackle Chad

Clifton after Tampa Bay cornerback Brian Kelly intercepted Favre in the third quarter.

"I just don't think there's any place in the game for that," Sherman said. "Maybe I overreacted to the hit. But what I saw looked kind of cheap. Who knows?"

Sherman's rant didn't matter much in the end. The Buccaneers went on to beat the Oakland Raiders – Gruden's former team – in Super Bowl XXXVII.

On the other hand, Brett Favre did an excellent job in December 2002. The Packers won four of their next five games to finish the year at 12-4. Favre had seven touchdown passes and three picks during that span. The Pack won the brand-new NFC North and the third seed in their conference. It meant they had home-field advantage in the Wild Card round against the Atlanta Falcons, Favre's former team.

Favre finished the regular season with 3,658 yards, 27 touchdown passes, and 16 interceptions. He earned his seventh Pro Bowl nod and fourth NFC Player of the Year Award. The NFL also named him for another Second Team All-Pro selection.

The NFC Wild Card Game between the Packers and Falcons took place at Lambeau Field on January 4, 2003. Green Bay wanted nothing more than to erase the stigma of its painful loss to the St. Louis Rams in the NFC Divisional Round a year earlier. It would be a challenging task. The Packers played without injured stars Ahman Green, Donald Driver, and Terry Glenn in the second half.

It turned out the odds were too much for Green Bay to overcome, even if the game was in front of 65,358 Cheeseheads.

Twenty-two-year-old Atlanta Falcons quarterback Michael Vick helped beat the veteran Favre and his Packers. Vick didn't have gaudy stats (he converted on 13 of 25 pass attempts for 117 yards and one touchdown, per PackersHistory.net), but his leadership was valuable. With him under center, Atlanta raced to a 24-0 halftime lead and never looked back. The Falcons prevailed, 24-7. The Packers were never in it and suffered their first home loss of the 2002 NFL season. Green Bay was going home again.

For his part, Brett Favre wound up with 247 yards, one touchdown, and two interceptions. His performance wasn't as bad as the one against the Rams the previous season.

Nonetheless, the results were the same. Favre and Co. had to regroup for the 2003 NFL season.

2003 NFL Season

Brett Favre and his Green Bay Packers had made it to two consecutive postseasons after not making it in 1999 and 2000. However, they were not able to go deep into the playoffs the following two seasons. In fact, the Pack lost badly to the St. Louis Rams (now the Los Angeles Rams) and Atlanta Falcons in 2001 and 2002, respectively.

It was a trend that Green Bay head coach and general manager Mike Sherman needed to stop.

Perhaps a fresh start would do the Packers a world of good. Their home stadium, Lambeau Field, underwent an offseason renovation.[lvii] A better stadium meant a better experience for the fans. In the end, it meant nothing if Brett Favre and Co. failed to play better in the postseason.

The Packers took on the Minnesota Vikings in their home opener at renovated Lambeau Field on September 7, 2003. The team rededicated its historic home at halftime.

Too bad Vikings wide receiver Randy Moss spoiled the party.

Moss had nine receptions for 150 yards and a touchdown in his team's 30-25 triumph. The sellout crowd of 70,505 went home disappointed.[lviii]

Green Bay tried to come back from a 27-3 deficit. Two goals from Ahman Green and one from Javon Walker inched the Pack to within five. However, they could not get any closer. Injuries to Donald Driver, Robert Ferguson, and Karsten Bailey were detrimental to Green Bay's cause. Favre got off to a bad start. He threw four interceptions (three in the first half) in the loss.

"I was upset we lost the game," Favre, who had 248 passing yards and one touchdown pass, told *The Associated Press*. "It was as ugly as it gets, but it wasn't anything Hovan did, or Randy Moss, or Daunte Culpepper, Mike Tice. No. There's no sense in being bitter with those guys. It's a great rivalry. I don't see why that should change. There's no ill feelings here."

Green Bay had a below-average first half of the season. The Packers went just 3-4 in their first seven games. One of those losses was to the Arizona Cardinals, who finished the 2003 NFL season with a terrible 4-12 win-loss record. Arizona beat Green Bay, 20-13, on September 21, 2003. Favre threw for 245 yards, one touchdown, and one interception in the sorry loss.[lix]

Fortunately, the Packers regrouped after their bye week. They won five of their next seven games to improve their record to 8-6. On November 2, 2003, Brett Favre's three touchdown passes helped Green Bay avenge their Week 1 loss to the Vikings. The Packers prevailed on the road, 30-27, per NFL.com.

While things had gone perfectly for Favre on the professional side, he suffered a major setback on the personal front.

His father, Irvin, died due to a stroke or heart attack while he was driving in Mississippi on December 22, 2003. His car went off the road and into a ditch. He died at 6:15 p.m. He was 58 years old, per *The Associated Press* (via *USA Today*).[lx]

Despite the setback, Favre told his teammates he would suit up for the Monday Night Football game against the Oakland Raiders on December 23. Before his father's death, he had started 204 straight games for the Packers – an NFL record – per *The Associated Press*.

Favre reiterated his desire to play to *Sports Illustrated's* Peter King. He said missing the game against Oakland was not an option.

"Never crossed my mind," Favre said. "What I do today is a direct result of his influence on my life. When I saw Mike

Sherman, he said, 'You want to go home, go.' I said, 'Mike, I'm playing. There's no doubt in my mind that's what he would have wanted.' It's almost like I could hear my dad, 'Boy, don't worry about me. I'm fine.'"[lxi]

According to King, "Favre hates giving speeches." However, he made an exception in the Packers' team meeting before the Raiders game. Favre was already in tears as he made his way to the front of the room. He struggled mightily to finish his speech. He told his teammates he loved his dad very much. He also assured them they had no reason to doubt his commitment to the Packers.

Sherman told *Sports Illustrated* everybody on the team cried after Favre's emotional speech. For his part, Favre admitted he was "scared" just before kickoff against Oakland. Sherman told his troops they were winning the game for Brett Favre and his father, Big Irv.

Favre started off hot – he connected on his first nine passes for 183 yards and two touchdowns, per King. He found his receivers despite double and triple coverage from the Oakland defense. He had thrown for 311 yards and four touchdowns in the first half alone. The 34-year-old Favre finished with 399 passing yards and four touchdown passes in the lopsided 41-7 win over the hapless Raiders.

It's as if Irvin Farve had smiled down from the sky.

Not only did Favre singlehandedly win the game for his father, he also brought the Packers back to playoff contention. According to *The Milwaukee Journal Sentinel's* Bob McGinn, the 9-6 Packers could win the NFC North if they beat the Denver Broncos and the Minnesota Vikings lose to the Arizona Cardinals the following week. Green Bay also established its best road record since 1972 (5-3) after the Oakland conquest.[lxii]

The Packers did their part. They blew out the Broncos, 31-3, on December 28, 2003. Surprisingly, the Cardinals upset the Vikings, 18-17. The Green Bay Packers were the 2003 NFC North champions.

Brett Favre threw for 3,361 yards, 32 touchdowns, and 21 interceptions in his 13th NFL season. Favre's 32 touchdown passes led the league – his fourth time to accomplish such a feat. He had thrown for at least 30 touchdowns for the seventh time in his career. Favre also earned his eighth Pro Bowl nod.

Because the Packers had the fewest wins among the NFC's four division champions, they got the fourth seed in the conference.

As a result, they faced the fifth-seeded Seattle Seahawks in the 2003 NFC Wild Card Game at Lambeau Field on January 4, 2004.

It was a thrilling game from start to finish.

Both teams scored two field goals in the first half. Favre's 23-yard touchdown pass to tight end Bubba Franks with four-and-a-half minutes left in the second quarter was the difference in the game's first 30 minutes. The Pack led at the half, 13-6.

Seattle Seahawks running back Shaun Alexander came to life in the second half. He scored two touchdowns in the third quarter to give his team the lead, 20-13. Packers running back Ahman Green countered with two goals within a seven-minute span in the fourth quarter for a 27-20 Packers lead. Alexander tied things up with his third touchdown run of the game with just 51 seconds remaining. Green Bay managed to march the football within field-goal range. Unfortunately, kicker Ryan Longwell missed a 47-yard attempt as time expired.

With four-and-a-half minutes gone by in overtime, Packers cornerback Al Harris intercepted Seattle quarterback Matt Hasselbeck's pass for a touchdown. Harris ran past Seahawks (and former Green Bay) head coach Mike Holmgren along the sideline. Harris' feat was the first overtime defensive touchdown to win an NFL playoff game, per PackersHistory.net. Final Score: Packers 33, Seahawks 27.

For his part, Brett Favre connected on 26 of 38 passes for 319 yards and one touchdown. His team had moved on to the NFC Divisional Round against the No.1- seeded Philadelphia Eagles at Lincoln Financial Field on January 11, 2004.

It was another exciting, heart-pounding game.

The Packers got the better of the Eagles in the first half. Favre collaborated with wide receiver Robert Ferguson for two touchdowns in the first quarter. The Eagles countered with quarterback Donovan McNabb's touchdown pass to running back Duce Staley in the second quarter. The visitors led at the halftime break, 14-7.

McNabb threw his second touchdown pass of the game when he connected with wide receiver Todd Pinkston early in the fourth quarter. Ryan Longwell's field goal four minutes later made it 17-14 for Green Bay. Neither team put points on the board for the next 10 minutes. Philadelphia was down to its last chance on 4th-and-26 with just 1:12 left to play. McNabb found wide receiver Freddie Mitchell for a key 28-yard completion. It set up David Akers' game-tying, 37-yard field goal at the end of regulation.

Eagles safety Brian Dawkins then intercepted Favre's pass early in overtime. McNabb and Co. methodically moved the sticks to set up David Akers' potential game-winning field goal with 4:48 gone by in the extra session. Akers' 31-yard field goal attempt sailed between the uprights. The Eagles had prevailed, 20-17. The Packers' season had ended in heartbreak once again.

Favre, who finished with 180 passing yards, two touchdowns, and one interception, did not speak with reporters after the game, per PackersHistory.net.

It had been seven years since Favre had last tasted victory in the Super Bowl. It had become a frustrating run for him ever since. He only hoped a string of consecutive postseason setbacks would finally result in a Super Bowl triumph in the 2004 NFL season.

2004 NFL Season

The Green Bay Packers had suffered three straight heartbreaking postseason losses. They had hoped the 2004 NFL season would be a better one for them. Their leading man, Brett Favre, was on the cusp of turning 35 years old. He had shown signs of aging and wear and tear in the previous years. It was a good thing he had resuscitated his career in the past few seasons.

Packers fans crossed their fingers the trend would continue in 2004.

Alas, the Pack got off to a miserable start. They won just one of their first five games. Nobody expected them to dig this deep of a hole so early in the season.

It grew worse for Green Bay.

Favre suffered a concussion in the third quarter of the game against the New York Giants on October 3, 2004. Giants defensive lineman William Joseph tackled him hard. Favre sat out the next two plays before returning on fourth down. Despite the concussion, he threw a 28-yard touchdown pass to Javon Walker for a 7-0 Packers lead. Favre even told his backup, Doug Pederson, to go back to the sideline, per *The Associated Press* (via ESPN).[lxiii] Favre wound up with 110 passing yards, one touchdown, and one interception in the 14-7 loss to New York.

Giants cornerback Terry Cousin paid homage to the Packers quarterback after the game.

"Brett Favre is Brett Favre," Cousin told *The Associated Press*. "We couldn't underestimate Doug Pederson. He's a good quarterback who's been in the league a long time. But only

Brett Favre can make some of those throws and make something out of nothing. That's the difference between him and everybody else."

New York defensive end Michael Strahan agreed with Cousin's assessment. He said he "wasn't surprised" Favre threw that touchdown pass to Walker.

The Green Bay Packers had a 1-3 record and a concussed Brett Favre after that game. Things did not look good.

All of a sudden, the football gods flipped a switch.

After a 48-27 loss to the Tennessee Titans on October 11, Green Bay won six straight games. The Packers took advantage of a soft schedule to put themselves back in playoff contention. Among the teams they faced during that six-game tear, only the Minnesota Vikings and St. Louis Rams sported a .500 record at the end of the season.

Brett Lorenzo Favre was his old MVP self again – he threw for 13 touchdowns and just two interceptions during the six-game winning streak.[lxiv] What concussion?

Favre's most memorable game during that season-changing run was a 34-31 triumph over the Minnesota Vikings at Lambeau

Field on November 14, 2004. Favre was fantastic, throwing for 236 yards, four touchdowns, and no interceptions.

Green Bay then tapered off, winning three of their last five games to finish the 2004 NFL season with a 10-6 win-loss record. One of the key games in the season's final stretch was against the Vikings on December 24. Favre recorded 365 passing yards, three touchdowns, and one interception in the 34-31 victory. The Packers had beaten the Vikings by the same score more than a month earlier. More importantly, the former clinched their third consecutive NFC North title with the win.

Favre owned up to his earlier mistake when he threw a pick-six to Minnesota linebacker Chris Claiborne on third down midway through the fourth quarter. It gave the Vikings a seven-point lead, 31-24. Almost five minutes later, Favre found Donald Driver in the end zone to tie things up once again. The Green Bay quarterback then led a late 76-yard drive which set up Ryan Longwell's game-winning 29-yard field goal.

The Packers showed resilience in becoming division champions again.

"Never give up," Favre told *The Associated Press* (via ESPN). "That's been this team's M.O. all season. Because we could've quit a long time ago."[lxv]

Favre was an epitome or resilience himself. He had suffered an early-season concussion against the Giants, threw 13 touchdown passes during a six-game run, and led the Pack to its third straight NFC North crown.

He finished the 2004 NFL season with 4,088 yards, 30 touchdowns, and 17 interceptions. It was his first time to throw for at least 4,000 yards since 1999, and it was also his eighth time to throw for at least 30 touchdowns in a season.

The third-seeded Packers earned the right to host the sixth-seeded Minnesota Vikings in the 2004 NFC Wild Card Game at Lambeau Field on January 9, 2005. Lo and behold, it was the upstart Vikings who stunned the Packers in the early going. Behind Daunte Culpepper's two touchdown passes and Morten Andersen's field goal in the first quarter, Minnesota raced to a 17-0 lead. Ryan Longwell's 43-yard field goal with less than three minutes left in the first quarter finally put Green Bay on the board. Favre, who struggled mightily during the game, threw a four-yard touchdown pass to tight end Bubba Franks early in the second quarter to make it 17-10 for the Vikings. Culpepper was undaunted. He threw his third touchdown pass of the game – this time to wide receiver Nate Burleson – at the halfway mark of the second quarter to give Minnesota a 14-point cushion.

Packers running back Najeh Davenport's one-yard touchdown run in the fourth quarter inched the Pack closer, 24-17. They still had life. However, Culpepper put an end to Green Bay's rally with his fourth touchdown pass. He found wide receiver Randy Moss – a long-time Green Bay nemesis – in the end zone for a 34-yard reception. It was also Moss' second touchdown haul of the game. The Packers' inability to contain Culpepper, Favre's struggles, and critical injuries to wide receivers Javon Walker and Robert Ferguson did them in.

Favre finished the game with 216 yards, one touchdown, and four interceptions, per NFL.com. He said almost everything went wrong in the loss to Minnesota.

"I'd like to think I'm a great quarterback," Favre told *The Associated Press* (via ESPN). "And I'm kidding myself if I think great quarterbacks don't have bad days. Bad throws. Bad reads. Or kickers don't miss kicks. Or good corners don't get beat. Or offensive linemen don't hold from time to time. But it seemed like all those things happened today."[lxvi]

The Packers' playoff futility had reached a fourth consecutive year. Their postseason fate became predictable with each passing year. If they didn't lose in the Wild Card Round, they would be out in the NFC Divisional Round. Brett Favre also had his share of playoff struggles. It was anybody's guess if the Pack could end this frustrating run. The Cheeseheads had grown increasingly weary.

2005 NFL Season

Things would become a whole lot worse for the Green Bay Packers in the 2005 NFL season. They lost offensive linemen Marco Rivera and Mike Wahle to free agency. An assortment of injuries would also dampen the Pack's hopes in 2005.

Management knew that Favre was clearly in decline. Because of this, the Packers drafted California Golden Bears quarterback Aaron Rodgers 24th overall in the 2005 NFL Draft.[lxvii]

The start of the 2005 NFL season was a virtual repeat of Green Bay's first five games the year before. They lost four of their first five contests with two of those coming at the expense of the Detroit Lions and Tampa Bay Buccaneers. The Lions won just five games while the Buccaneers won only six games in 2005.

The Packers finally broke into the win column with a 52-3 rout of the hapless New Orleans Saints on October 9, 2005. Hurricane Katrina – one of the worst natural disasters in United States history – displaced the Saints from their city a month-and-a-half earlier. New Orleans would also suffer through a very long season. The Saints finished the year with an abysmal 3-13 win-loss record. The injury bug also bit the Pack in the game against New Orleans. They lost running back Najeh Davenport to an ankle injury in the second quarter. He would not play again in the 2005 NFL season. He joined the likes of Mike Flanagan, Javon Walker, Ahman Green, and Buffa Franks in the Packers' injured reserve.

Favre, who threw for 215 yards, three touchdowns, and no interceptions, told *The Associated Press* (via ESPN) it was a crucial win for his team.

"That's the first time I've ever played in a game where we scored 50 points," he quipped. "Who would've guessed it? We're 0-4, struggling, more guys hurt and even lose guys during the course of the game. But I've played long enough to know that if you do things the right way, if you study, prepare, and believe, things will go your way."[lxviii]

Remember, the Packers regrouped in time to salvage their 2004 NFL season. After they had gone 1-4, they won six in a row on their way to a third NFC North division title.

It would be completely different in 2005.

Green Bay went 3-8 in its last 11 games to finish with an appalling 4-12 win-loss record. It was their worst showing since the 1991 NFL season when they won the same number of games.[lxix] They also missed the postseason for the first time since 2000.

According to PackersHistory.net, the lack of a solid ground game was one of the reasons for the 4-12 showing in 2005. Green Bay utilized a total of seven running backs that season: Ahman Green, Najeh Davenport, Tony Fisher, Samkon Gado, Noah Herron, Walt Williams, and Rashard Lee. No matter how hard the Packers tried, they just could not find the player who could shore up their running attack.

For his part, Brett Favre, who suffered through his first losing season, was not any better.

He threw for 3,881 yards, 20 touchdowns, and a career-low 29 interceptions, per NFL.com. His 70.9 passer rating placed him 31st among NFL quarterbacks[lxx]. It was the worst of his 15-year NFL career. Apparently, the lack of a reliable offensive line and wide receivers affected his game severely.

Brett Favre's miserable year prompted him to bring up the possibility of retirement.

"I wish I knew where I stood," Favre told ESPN's Chris Mortensen in a January 21, 2006, interview at his home in Mississippi. "If I had to pick right now and make a decision, I would say I'm not coming back."[lxxi]

Favre told Mortensen he needed more time to weigh his options. He should have made a decision before training camp kicked off in late July 2006.

On the other hand, Packers general manager Ted Thompson fired head coach Mike Sherman on January 2, 2006. Thompson stressed that he dismissed Sherman because he felt he was not the right fit for the team's long-term future, per *The Associated Press* (via ESPN).[lxxii] Sherman concluded his six-year stint with the Packers with a 57-39 (.594) win-loss record.[lxxiii]

Six years later, former Packers president Bob Harlan told ESPN Milwaukee (via NFL.com's Marc Sessler) that making Sherman the team's head coach and general manager in 2001 "the worst decision I made."[lxxiv]

Ten days later, the Packers hired 42-year-old Mike McCarthy as the 14th head coach in franchise history, *per The Milwaukee Journal Sentinel's* Bob McGinn. McCarthy, a 13-year NFL coaching veteran, previously served as the offensive coordinator of the New Orleans Saints and San Francisco 49ers. He was also

Brett Favre's quarterbacks coach in the 1999 NFL season. His return to Green Bay marked his first head coaching stint in the pro ranks. McCarthy signed a three-year, $6 million contract.[lxxv]

"I am blessed to be here, clearly the grace of God," McCarthy told McGinn. "I want to tell you how comfortable through the whole process that I felt. Not to sound overconfident, but I am just thrilled to have the opportunity to come back here."

Although McCarthy was excited to be back in Green Bay, he was in a tough spot. He had to resurrect a woebegone franchise which had just come off a 4-12 season. If Brett Favre did not return for his 16th season, it would become even more challenging.

2006 NFL Season

Three months after he told ESPN he had been leaning toward retirement, Brett Favre declared that he would return for the 2006 NFL season.

"The Green Bay Packers are very pleased that Brett has come to this decision, and look forward to a successful 2006 season," general manager Ted Thompson said in a statement which ESPN obtained on April 26, 2006.[lxxvi]

At the time of Favre's decision, he was second to Dan Marino in passing yards, touchdowns, and completions, per ESPN. Favre had 53,615 passing yards while Marino had 61,361 passing yards. That meant it would have taken Favre three more seasons to surpass the great Marino. If there were anyone in the NFL who could do it, it was Brett Favre.

Now that he was officially back, a big question loomed: Would he be able to co-exist with his new head coach, Mike McCarthy? The two worked for a year in the 1999 NFL season when McCarthy was the Pack's quarterbacks coach. The 2006 NFL season was a different story. McCarthy now called the shots for Green Bay. He had to establish a good relationship with his quarterback. He had laid the foundation seven years earlier, and it was time to build on it.

Unfortunately, McCarthy's NFL head coaching stint didn't get off to a good start. For the third year in a row, the Packers stumbled out of the gate. They went just 1-4 in their first five games. During that period, Green Bay lost to the Chicago Bears and Philadelphia Eagles by 26 points and 22 points, respectively. Chicago and Philadelphia were both playoff-bound teams in 2006. Favre was not spectacular. He threw for seven touchdowns and five interceptions during that five-game stretch.

At that point, there was no indication that he could shake off the stigma of his 29-interception season in 2005.

Thankfully, the Packers regrouped and won three of their four games after their bye week. Two of those victories were against the Miami Dolphins and Arizona Cardinals, who won just six games and five games, respectively, in the 2006 NFL season.

On November 12, 2006, Favre threw for 347 yards, two touchdowns, and no interceptions in a pivotal 23-17 road win over the Minnesota Vikings. Green Bay wide receiver Donald Driver caught for a career-high 191 yards in the win.

Favre, who celebrated his 37th birthday the previous month, played loosely against the Vikings. After Favre had thrown a five-yard touchdown pass to Green Bay wide receiver Noah Herron early in the first quarter, he leaped into the latter's arms and gave him a pat on his shoulder, per *The Associated Press* (via ESPN).[lxxvii]

The victory upped the Packers' win-loss record to 4-5. Favre also improved his record against the Vikings at the Hubert H. Humphrey Metrodome to 5-10.

The Packers continued to swing like a pendulum during the 2006 NFL season. After they had beaten Minnesota, they lost three in a row to playoff contenders the New England Patriots, Seattle Seahawks, and New York Jets by an average of almost 28 points. Green Bay continued beating sub-par teams and losing to excellent ones.

For his part, Favre was terrible during the three-game skid. He threw just two touchdown passes and threw the ball away five times. It was a result of an elbow injury he sustained in the second quarter of the Packers' embarrassing 35-0 shutout loss to the Patriots at Lambeau Field on November 19, 2006. Favre's second-year backup, Aaron Rogers, wasn't any better, converting on just 4 of 12 passes for 32 yards. According *to The Associated Press* (via ESPN), witnesses saw Rodgers limping in the locker room after the game. It was an awful sign for Mike McCarthy and Co.[lxxviii]

It seemed the 4-8 Green Bay Packers were down for the count.

However, they somehow came up with a strong late-season push. Green Bay went on a four-game winning streak, capped off by a 26-7 road win over the Chicago Bears on New Year's Eve (the Bears would later lose to the Indianapolis Colts in Super Bowl XLI). Favre threw for two touchdown passes and six interceptions during the four-game run.

He finished the 2006 NFL season with 3,885 passing yards, 18 touchdown passes, and 18 interceptions. Although he did gain on Marino in the NFL's all-time passing yardage list, the Packers finished with a mediocre 8-8 mark, which was good for second in the NFC North division. They missed the postseason for the second consecutive year. Could Favre have played his last down in the NFL?

"If this is the last game, I couldn't be more pleased with the outcome," a teary-eyed Favre told PackersHistory.net after the win over the Bears. "If this is my last game, I want to remember it. It's tough. I love these guys. I love this game. What a great way to go out against a great football team. I couldn't ask for a better way to get out."[lxxix]

Favre, who was set to undergo ankle surgery on January 1, 2007, told PackersHistory.net that he needed a few weeks to mull things over with his family. Favre had not been as sharp as he had been the past two seasons. Nevertheless, with an improved roster in 2007, the Pack could boost their chances of ending their short playoff drought. Their fans could only wait for Brett Favre to make another pivotal decision.

2007 NFL Season

The Green Bay Packers got off to a mediocre start in the Mike McCarthy era. They had finished 8-8 in 2006 and fell out of playoff contention for the second year in a row. However, they had to look at the bright side: It was a four-game improvement from the season before. It was hard to imagine the team making a 360-degree turnaround with an aging Brett Favre and a less-than-stellar supporting cast.

The first thing Green Bay had to know was if Favre was coming back for his 17th pro season. After the 26-7 win over the Chicago Bears in the 2006 season finale, Favre gave strong indications that it could have been his last NFL game.

Not so fast.

On February 2, 2007 – just two days before Super Bowl XLI between the Indianapolis Colts and Chicago Bears (which the Colts won, 29-17) – Favre announced that he would return.

"I am so excited about coming back," Favre told PackersHistory.net. "We have a good nucleus of young players. We were 8-8 last year, and that's encouraging."[lxxx]

The Packers re-signed tight end Donald Lee, defensive lineman Cullen Jenkins, and running back Noah Herron. They also added linebacker Desmond Bishop, kicker Mason Crosby, wide receiver James Jones, and running back Ryan Grant. Grant's acquisition was meant to offset the loss of Ahman Green, who signed with the Houston Texans. It was a very busy offseason for Green Bay general manager Ted Thompson.

There were also rumors the Packers were interested in former Minnesota Vikings wide receiver and long-time Green Bay nemesis Randy Moss. However, the New England Patriots wound up signing the 30-year-old in exchange for a fourth-round draft pick on April 29, 2007. Favre reportedly wanted Moss so badly that he told his agent after the 2007 NFL Draft that he wanted the Packers to trade him. Fortunately, head coach Mike McCarthy was able to pacify Favre over the phone, per PackersHistory.net.

Despite losing out on Moss, Green Bay got off to a scintillating start in the 2007 NFL season. The Pack won five of their first six games before their bye week. They beat playoff contenders the New York Giants and San Diego Chargers in Week 2 and Week 3. Favre had nine touchdown passes and six interceptions in Green Bay's first six games in 2007.[lxxxi]

Favre's most memorable game of the season's first half was the 35-13 conquest of the Giants on September 16, 2007. By winning his 149th game, Favre became the winningest quarterback in NFL history. He had just surpassed former Denver Broncos signal caller John Elway. Favre also closed in on Dan Marino's all-time passing record after the former threw for 286 yards in the win over New York. Favre had amassed 57,992 passing yards, while Marino finished his NFL career with 61,361 yards, per ESPN.[lxxxii]

Favre's teammates handed the game ball to him after the victory. He told ESPN that it was something he would cherish.

"I'm not going to sit here and lie to you," he said. "I'm not going to turn it down. I've always been about the team. That hasn't changed. I think it's unfair that the quarterback gets labeled with wins and losses. I think it's a team effort."

Two weeks later, Favre reached another milestone against the Minnesota Vikings.

His 16-yard touchdown pass to Donald Driver in the first quarter was the 421st in his NFL career. It enabled him to surpass Marino. Favre padded his lead when he threw a touchdown strike to rookie James Jones in the fourth quarter. The Green Bay quarterback had 344 yards, two touchdowns, and no interceptions in the 23-16 win. The Packers also improved their record to 4-0.

Favre continued to pile up on the accolades.

He became just the third quarterback after Tom Brady and Peyton Manning to beat the other 31 NFL teams after a 33-22 win over the Kansas City Chiefs on November 4, 2007. His key 60-yard touchdown pass to wide receiver Greg Jennings with 3:05 remaining proved to be the difference. Favre connected on 24 of 34 passes for 360 yards, two touchdowns, and two interceptions. After the game, Favre conceded that teams such as the New England Patriots and Indianapolis Colts were better than the Packers. However, he emphasized that their 7-1 record "speaks for itself." He lauded his team's ability to improvise and win games at critical junctures.[lxxxiii]

Green Bay never lost its mojo after the bye week. The Pack won eight of their last ten games to finish with a 13-3 record – their best mark since the 1997 NFL season. The Packers had turned a corner. A revitalized Brett Favre and a better supporting cast were the keys to their impressive turnaround. Green Bay won the NFC North and earned the second seed in their conference, which meant they had home-field advantage in the 2007 NFC Divisional Round.

Favre finished the 2007 NFL season with 4,155 passing yards – his fifth time to pass for at least 4,000 yards in a season. He also had 28 touchdown passes and 15 interceptions, per NFL.com. It was a stunning turnaround from his past few seasons

What was the difference? Favre's backup, Aaron Rodgers (who would later lead the Packers to victory over the Pittsburgh Steelers in Super Bowl XLV), told *Sports Illustrated's* Peter King in December 2007 that Favre had become a more vocal leader.

"(Brett's) become a lot more vocal, a lot more hands-on," Rodgers said. "He's out there coaching the entire offense, from running back to wide receiver to tight end. In practice, he'll break away from what (the quarterbacks) are doing to watch some of the other positions go through their reps. He's extremely engaged in everything that's happening."[lxxxiv]

Favre earned his ninth Pro Bowl nod, third Second Team All-Pro Selection, and fifth NFC Player of the Year Award in 2007. He had revived his once-sagging NFL career.

The 2007 NFC Divisional Round Game between the Green Bay Packers and Seattle Seahawks took place at Lambeau Field on January 12, 2008. Green Bay had beat Seattle, 33-27, the last time the two teams met in the postseason. Al Harris intercepted Matt Hasselbeck for a touchdown in overtime in the 2003 NFC

Wild Card Game. Four years later, the Seahawks wanted payback.

It was a close game in the first half. The Seahawks established a 14-0 lead in the first quarter after a one-year Shaun Alexander run and an 11-yard touchdown pass from Hasselbeck to Bobby Engram. In the Packers' last two postseason stints, they had a history of collapsing. Not on this day. They countered with Greg Jennings' 15-yard touchdown reception and Ryan Grant's one-yard touchdown run to tie things up. Favre's second pass to Jennings in the end zone early in the second quarter gave Green Bay the lead, 21-14. Four minutes later, Seattle's Josh Brown converted on a 29-yard field goal to trim the deficit to four at the half.

The Packers' balanced attack on offense and their tight defense made the difference in the final 30 minutes.

Grant's second touchdown run of the game increased Green Bay's lead to 11 early in the third quarter. Favre recorded his third touchdown pass when he connected with Brandon Jackson 10 minutes later for a commanding 35-17 lead after the extra point. Grant finished off the Seahawks for good with his third touchdown run of the game in the opening moments of the fourth quarter. The Seahawks scored just three points in the entire second half. Final Score: Green Bay 42, Seattle 20.

Favre connected on 18 of 23 passes for 173 yards, three touchdowns, and no interceptions in an efficient performance, per PackersHistory.net.

The Pack were now just two wins away from winning another Super Bowl. They took on Eli Manning and the New York Giants in the 2007 NFC Championship Game at Lambeau Field on January 20, 2008. It was so cold in Green Bay that PackersHistory.net described the wind chill as something "that would make a Siberian husky shiver." In fact, it was the third-coldest conference championship game in league history.

The Giants got on the board first with two Lawrence Tynes field goals for a 6-0 lead. The Packers came right back with a Brett Favre touchdown pass to Donald Driver with 3:19 gone by in the second quarter. Rookie kicker Mason Crosby made a 36-yard field goal with 90 seconds remaining in the first half to make it 10-6 for the Packers.

The Giants' running game came to life in the third quarter. Brandon Jacobs scored on a one-yard run with just over seven minutes left in the quarter. Five-and-a-half minutes later, Ahmad Bradshaw got into the end zone. And three minutes earlier, Favre threw his second touchdown pass of the game. It was Donald Lee's turn to haul the football in for the Packers. It was 20-17 for the Giants after 45 minutes of action.

In Green Bay's ensuing possession, Favre threw a desperation pass which Giants cornerback R.W. McQuarters intercepted. Fortunately for the Packers, McQuarters fumbled after running back Ryan Grant tackled him. Green Bay tackle Mark Tauscher recovered the football.

Tynes had his chances to win the game for the Giants in the fourth quarter. However, he bungled two field-goal tries. He missed a 43-yard attempt and a 36-yarder at the end of regulation.

The Packers won the coin toss to kick off the overtime session. Unfortunately, Favre threw another interception. It was Giants cornerback Corey Webster's turn to pick him off. New York quarterback Eli Manning – who finished with 251 passing yards – orchestrated a crucial drive in overtime. He helped move the sticks to set up Tynes' potential game-winning 47-yard field goal attempt.

Tynes shook off the sting of his two earlier misses to nail the one which counted the most. The New York Giants were moving on to Super Bowl XLII against the undefeated New

England Patriots on February 3, 2008. The Green Bay Packers were going home.

Favre, who wound up with 236 passing yards, two touchdowns, and two interceptions, told *The Associated Press* (via ESPN)that he was mad at himself for his costly interception in overtime.

"I was disappointed that the last pass I threw was intercepted," Favre said. "For me, I kept thinking how many opportunities are we going to let slip away."[lxxxv]

Once again, the million-dollar question loomed for Cheeseheads across the country: Had Brett Favre played his last down in Packers Gold and Green?

2008 NFL Season

After several up-and-down seasons with the Green Bay Packers in the past few years, Brett Lorenzo Favre dropped a bombshell on the football world in March 2008: He announced his retirement, per PackersHistory.net.[lxxxvi] Two weeks afterward, he toyed with the idea of returning, but changed his mind. Favre continued to be fickle-minded. On June 20, he told Packers head coach Mike McCarthy that he might suit up for Green Bay.

Favre then filed a request for reinstatement to active status with the National Football League on July 29, 2008. Five days later,

McCarthy and Co. welcomed their legendary signal caller to training camp. However, Favre could not reach a compromise with the Packers during a five-hour meeting the following day. Both sides agreed to mutually part ways. Rumors had it that Favre was heading to the Tampa Bay Buccaneers, but that did not materialize. Green Bay had traded him to the New York Jets on August 7, 2008, per PackersHistory.net.

Green Bay president and CEO Mark Murphy and executive vice president, general manager, and director of football operations Ted Thompson issued a joint statement on Packers.com regarding the Favre trade. They said they owed Favre "a tremendous debt of gratitude for everything he accomplished on the field and for the impact he made on the state." They expressed sadness at his departure, but also optimism because they felt that they had made the move with the team's best interests in mind. They added they respected Favre's decision to leave the organization. However, Murphy and Thompson said that they did not want to release or trade Favre to an NFC North division rival. They also wished Favre and his family well. He left as the NFL's all-time leader in touchdowns (442), yards (61,655), completions (5,377), and attempts (8,758).[lxxxvii]

According to ESPN, the Packers traded Favre to the Jets for a conditional draft pick (it was initially fourth-round draft choice which became a third-rounder after Favre took 50 percent of total snaps with the Jets in the 2008 NFL season). Green Bay also made sure the Minnesota Vikings would not be able to get Brett Favre. Had the latter done so, the Jets would have to give up three first-round draft picks to the Packers, per NFL Network (via ESPN). Favre's arrival also meant Chad Pennington's days in New York were over. Pennington was the Jets' starting quarterback in 2007 when they posted an abysmal 4-12 record. He signed with the Miami Dolphins in the offseason. [lxxxviii]

Favre got off to a good start with the Jets. He threw for two touchdowns in their 20-14 Week 1 victory over their AFC East rivals, the Miami Dolphins, on September 8, 2008. It was the Jets' fifth consecutive win over Miami. Favre made an immediate impact on the Jets' second series of the game – he threw a 56-yard touchdown to wide receiver Jerricho Cotchery for a 7-0 New York lead. According to *The Associated Press* (via ESPN), Favre "celebrated like a rookie" after the play.[lxxxix]

Favre struck again in the second quarter. He threw a fourth-down pass under heavy defensive pressure which Jets wide receiver Chansi Stuckey caught for the go-ahead score.

Favre told *The Associated Press* (via ESPN) after the game that he was happy to be in The Big Apple.

"I know I made the right decision," he said. "I'm a New York Jet. I don't know about a native New Yorkian, or however you say it. Hey, I'm happy to be a Jet."

The Jets then lost two in a row before beating the Arizona Cardinals in a high-scoring affair on September 28, 2008. Favre rediscovered his youthful touch when he threw for 289 yards, six touchdowns, and just one interception in the 56-35 triumph. Favre's six touchdowns (he threw three to wide receiver Laveranues Coles) tied the franchise record which legendary quarterback Joe Namath held previously. It was even more impressive because Favre was nursing a sore ankle.[xc]

The Jets won six of their next seven games after their bye week. After their 16-13 overtime loss to the Oakland Raiders on October 19, 2008, they beat the Kansas City Chiefs, Buffalo Bills, St. Louis Rams, New England Patriots, and Tennessee Titans. At that point, New York looked impressive with an 8-3 win-loss record. Favre had thrown for 20 touchdowns and 13 interceptions during the Jets' tear.[xci]

Without a doubt, the Jets' best moment of the season was on November 23, 2008. After they had beaten the Patriots a week earlier, they blew out the previously unbeaten Titans, 34-13. New York led at the half, 10-3. They never looked back in handing Tennessee their first setback. Favre threw for 224 yards, two touchdowns, and one interception in the win. He had lost his first game at LP Field when he was still a member of the Green Bay Packers in 2001.

"I'm not going to sit here and say we've established ourselves as the best team in football," Favre told *The Associated Press* (via ESPN). "All it says I think we beat the best team in football today; definitely, if you go by record and the way that they've played. They have been the best team in football."[xcii]

The bottom then fell out on Jets after the win over the Titans.

Just when New York needed to play well to solidify a postseason berth, the team lost four of its last five games. Brett Favre was lackluster, throwing for just two touchdowns and nine interceptions as the Jets kissed their playoff hopes goodbye. They did finish with a 9-7 mark, but it was not enough.

To make matters worse, their final loss of the season came at the expense of their former quarterback, Chad Pennington. He threw for 200 yards, two touchdowns, and no interceptions in the 24-17 win over New York on December 28, 2008. The victory clinched the AFC East for the 11-5 Dolphins.

For his part, Brett Favre threw for 233 yards, a touchdown, and no interceptions. Favre told *The Associated Press* (via ESPN) he would undergo an MRI on his injured right shoulder on December 29. It had been bothering him for some time.[xciii] He finished the 2008 NFL season with 3,472 yards, 22 touchdowns, and 22 interceptions, per NFL.com.[xciv] He also earned his 10th Pro Bowl selection.

A week after the loss to the Dolphins, Favre told *Sports Illustrated's* Peter King (via ESPN) that the MRI revealed a damaged right bicep. The 39-year-old quarterback also told Jets general manager Mike Tannenbaum "it may be time to look in a different direction" as a result. Tannenbaum told Favre to take his time in mulling over his future with the team.[xcv]

On February 11, 2009, Favre made his decision. He announced his retirement for a second time, per *The New York Times'* Greg Bishop.[xcvi]

Favre told Bishop he would have considered playing in the 2009 NFL season had he been in good health. He had not, so he felt it was time to hang up his cleats.

"I got my answer as the season progressed. I finally can't throw the ball like I once threw it," he told *The New York Times*. "You name it in professional football; I've done that. Very few people, if any, can say that. I wouldn't trade my career for anything."

The Jets released Favre from their reserved-retired list on April 29, 2009. It made him a free agent, eligible to sign with any team should he come out of retirement.[xcvii]

It turned out that Brett Lorenzo Favre was not done with football yet. Not by a long shot.

2009 NFL Season

It had been a crazy past few seasons for Brett Favre. He had suffered through a 4-12 season with the Packers in 2005. He led a rejuvenated Green Bay squad to a 13-3 win-loss mark and an appearance in the 2007 NFC Championship Game two years later. He retired, un-retired, and then signed with the New York Jets. After a disappointing one-year stint in the Big Apple, he retired once again.

His next move would sting Green Bay Packers fans of all generations.

According to *The Milwaukee Journal Sentinel's* Lori Nickel, Favre un-retired yet again and signed with one of the Packers' fiercest rivals – the Minnesota Vikings – on August 18, 2009.[xcviii]

Brett Lorenzo Favre, the heart and soul of the Green Bay Packers franchise for 16 seasons, was now a Minnesota Viking.

Favre told Nickel he had an injured rotator cuff in his right shoulder. However, his doctors said it would not affect him that much. He set aside his retirement plans when Vikings head coach Brad Childress called him. An ESPN report (via *The Milwaukee Journal Sentinel*) revealed Favre signed a two-year, $25 million contract with Minnesota. He would earn $12 million in 2009 and $13 million in 2010.

Favre insisted his latest move had nothing to do with revenge against the Packers, per Nickel.

"Sixteen years in Green Bay were great years, and that was home to me," he said. "And some great games against this organization, some we won, some we lost...This is not about revenge, believe me. You can't take away the 16 years in Green Bay, and that will be forever cherished."

"They've moved on, I've moved on," he continued. "I think it's great for football. I can't see how you wouldn't think it would be."

For his part, Packers head coach Mike McCarthy told *The Milwaukee Journal* Sentinel that he wasn't surprised at the turn of events.

None of the Packers' fans' opinions would have mattered anymore. Brett Favre had made up his mind. He would spend the twilight of his National Football League career in Eden Prairie, Minnesota.

With stalwarts such as quarterback Gus Frerotte, running back Adrian Peterson, and wide receiver Bernard Berrian, the Vikings finished with a 10-6 win-loss record in 2008. Unfortunately, they lost to the Philadelphia Eagles in the 2008 NFC Wild Card Game, 26-14. Minnesota wanted to build on its success. Thirty-nine-year-old (and almost 40-year-old) Brett Favre would be their starting quarterback in the 2009 NFL season.

Favre started the year looking like anything but a has-been.

He won his first game as a member of the Purple and Gold as the Minnesota Vikings edged the Cleveland Browns, 34-20, on September 15, 2009. Favre recorded his first touchdown pass as a Viking with 1:12 left in the third quarter. He connected with rookie wide receiver Percy Harvin for six yards and a 23-13 lead. Adrian Peterson added 180 rushing yards and three touchdowns for the Vikings.

"I had a blast," Favre told *The Associated Press* (via ESPN). "It wasn't a 400-yard passing game, but it doesn't have to be. As long as we win, that's what it's all about."[xcix]

After beating Cleveland, the Vikings beat the Detroit Lions and San Francisco 49ers to extend their streak to three games. It set the stage for the much-awaited Week 4 game against Favre's old team – the Green Bay Packers – on October 5, 2009.

Favre continued to defy the odds when he connected on 24 of 31 passes for 271 yards, three touchdowns, and no interceptions in the 30-23 win over Green Bay. As a result, he became the first quarterback in history to defeat all 32 NFL teams. The last team he conquered proved to be the sweetest win of them all.

The Vikings' defense also played a big factor in the win, Minnesota's fourth straight. The Vikings sacked Favre's former backup, Aaron Rodgers, eight times (linebacker Jared Allen accounted for 4.5 sacks). Favre gave Rodgers, Donald Driver, and several other former teammates hugs at the end of the game. Favre also told *The Associated Press* (via ESPN) that he was as nervous before this game as he was before the memorable 399-yard, four-touchdown performance against the Oakland Raiders on Monday Night Football in December 2003.ᶜ It was the day after his father Irvin Favre died.

Favre would face the Packers again a month afterward. The game on November 2, 2009, marked the first time he played at Green Bay's Lambeau Field wearing an opposing uniform. Would he be able to make it 2-0 against his former team?

Yes, he would. He was sharp once again, throwing for 244 yards, four touchdowns, and no interceptions in the 38-26 road win.

The Vikings established a 17-3 lead at the half. Favre, who had battled shoulder issues the previous season, threw a 51-yard touchdown pass to wide receiver Percy Harvin with just 1:40 gone by in the third quarter for a commanding 24-3 advantage. More impressively, Favre threaded the needle in triple coverage. As soon as Harvin caught the football, the three Green Bay defenders – Charles, Woodson, Atari Bigby, and Nick Collins – fell to the ground. Packers quarterback Aaron Rodgers threw two second-half touchdown passes as he tried to lead a comeback. However, it fell short. The Minnesota defense had been dominant again, sacking Rodgers six times.

According to *The Associated Press* (via ESPN), Packers fans "booed Favre loudly." Cheeseheads jeered him every time they had a chance. As he walked off the field after the victory, he pumped his fist to a mixed reaction from the sellout crowd at Lambeau Field.[ci]

"Packers fans cheer for the Packers first," the 40-year-old Favre quipped. "I know that. But I hope that everyone in the stadium watching tonight said, 'I sure hate those jokers on the other side, but he does play the way he's always played.'"

At that point, the Vikings had won seven of eight games overall before their bye week on November 8, 2009. They would win five of their next eight games to finish with an impressive 12-4 mark, a four-game improvement from the year before. They earned the second seed in the NFC. It meant they drew a first-round bye and had home-field advantage in the 2009 NFC Divisional Round.

Favre saved his best for last when he recorded a scintillating performance against the New York Giants in the Vikings' season finale. He threw for 316 yards, four touchdowns, and no interceptions in the 44-7 rout of Eli Manning and Co. on January 3, 2010. He finished the 2009 NFL season with 4,202 yards, 33 touchdowns, and just seven interceptions – the fewest he had ever thrown in his 18-year NFL career. Favre also threw for at least 30 touchdowns for the ninth time. He also topped the

4,000-yard mark for the sixth time.[cii] Lastly, he played in his 11th Pro Bowl game. Not bad for a 40-year-old.

The Vikings took on quarterback Tony Romo and the Dallas Cowboys in the 2009 NFC Divisional Round at the Humphrey Metrodome on January 17, 2010. The Cowboys beat the Philadelphia Eagles, 34-14, in the 2009 NFC Wild Card Game to advance against Minnesota. Romo would get a taste of how dominant the Vikings' defense was. A rejuvenated Brett Favre would also torch the Cowboys.

Minnesota sacked Romo six times, and Favre continued his tear with a four-touchdown performance (three to wide receiver Sidney Rice). He connected on 15 of 24 passes for 234 yards. He also became the first 40-year-old quarterback to win a playoff game. It was never close. The Vikings routed the Cowboys, 34-3.[ciii] Minnesota advanced to their first NFC Championship Game in nine years.

The 2009 NFC Championship Game between the Minnesota Vikings and New Orleans Saints took place at the Louisiana Superdome on January 24, 2010. It would prove to be an exciting contest.

Vikings running back Adrian Peterson put his team on the board first with a 19-yard touchdown run with 9:41 left in the first quarter. Ryan Longwell's successful point after touchdown (PAT) made it 7-0 for Minnesota. Three minutes later, the Saints would come right back with a Drew Brees 38-yard touchdown pass to running back Pierre Thomas. Favre countered with a 5-yard touchdown strike to Sidney Rice at the 2:16 mark. The Vikings led after 15 minutes of play, 14-7.

The pace slowed down considerably in the second quarter. The Saints went on a seven-play, 64-yard drive capped off by a nine-yard Devery Henderson touchdown reception to tie things up at 14. It was a defensive stalemate afterward. Both squads alternated punts before Favre fumbled at the Saints' 10-yard line with a minute left to play in the half. New Orleans Saints linebacker Scott Fujita recovered for his team. The score was 14-14 at the half.

After New Orleans had spotted the ball on the Vikings' 37-yard line to begin the third quarter, Drew Brees found tight end David Thomas for a 17-yard gain on first down. The Saints kept pounding the ball on the ground until running back Pierre Thomas found the end zone at the 13:05 mark of the third quarter. Minnesota would not relent. The Vikings went on a methodical nine-play, 90-yard drive which ended with a one-yard touchdown from Peterson. The score was tied yet again.

Vikings backup quarterback Sage Rosenfels described the brutal nature of the game to MMQB.com's Peter King on August 7, 2013.

"Every play felt like a fourth down," Rosenfels quipped. "Brett was playing unbelievably well while taking lots of shots, legal and illegal. He kept our team together, moving the offense up and down the field while making very few mistakes. Still, the raw physical brutality was unprecedented in anything I had seen in my nine-year career. There had been rumors during the week the Saints' plan was to take Brett out of the game, and the hits started to wear on him mentally and physically. By the fourth quarter, he had a badly swollen left wrist, a deep scratch on his forehead, ribs that were in pain whenever he took a breath and a badly sprained ankle which could easily have been broken."[civ]

The turning point came early in the fourth quarter when Vikings wide receiver Percy Harvin fumbled at their seven-yard line. The Saints recovered and regained the lead on a Reggie Bush touchdown run on third down. Officials initially ruled Bush was out of bounds at the one-yard line. However, Saints head coach Sean Peyton threw out the red challenge flag. The officials upheld his challenge and the touchdown.

The Vikings remained undaunted. Peterson connected with tight end Visanthe Shiancoe for a 16-yard gain on the ensuing series. Peterson gained another 20 yards on the ground. The officials then flagged Saints cornerback Tracy Porter for pass interference. Peterson scored his third touchdown of the game moments later for yet another deadlock.

Fortunately for Minnesota, New Orleans went three and out on its ensuing series. Favre threw a bullet to Sidney Rice, which moved the line of scrimmage near the 50-yard line with just 1:39 left in the game. According to Rosenfels, it "got crazy on our sideline" after that play. All Favre and Co. had to do were melt the clock and move the ball within field-goal range for a trip to Super Bowl XLIV.

The Vikings reached field-goal range, but could not get any closer on first and second down. To make matters worse, they had 12 players on the field with 19 seconds left. The officials penalized them five yards. On the ensuing third-down play, Favre had a chance to scramble and run. However, he changed his mind and threw the ball to Rice.

Unfortunately, Saints cornerback Tracy Porter stepped into the passing lane and intercepted Favre's pass. He almost ran it back for a touchdown. The Vikings were lucky he wasn't able to. The game was going into overtime.

The Saints won the coin toss in overtime. A disgruntled Favre walked over to the sideline and sat right next to Rosenfels. Favre said, "I choked."

It took New Orleans 10 plays to march the football 39 yards and reach Minnesota's 22-yard line. Saints kicker Garrett Hartley nailed the game-winning 40-yard field goal with 4:41 gone by in the extra session. Final score: New Orleans 31, Minnesota 28. The Saints had moved on to Super Bowl XLIX to face the Indianapolis Colts in Miami, Fl. Brett Favre and his Minnesota Vikings were going home.

A battered Favre, who had grown up a Saints fan in Mississippi, poured out his emotions to ESPN after the game.

"I would have loved to represent the NFC," he quipped. "But, as I told (Saints head coach) Sean (Payton) throughout the year when we talked, if it's not us, I hope it's you guys."[cv]

Favre was so close to winning his second Super Bowl ring. Unfortunately, it was not meant to be. Would he be able to defy Father Time and accomplish this with the Vikings in the 2010 NFL season? It made for an interesting and juicy storyline.

2010 NFL Season

As the 2010 NFL season approached, Brett Lorenzo Favre was in his usual predicament. Would he retire or play another year? If he did, it would mark his 20th in the National Football League. He was on the verge of turning 41 years old. His performance in the 2009 NFL season was an indication that he could still play quarterback the game's highest level. He still had it.

Favre couldn't get over the painful overtime loss to the New Orleans Saints in the 2009 NFC Championship Game. It was one of the reasons which spurred him to play one more season. Favre made it official on August 20, 2010 – he would be back for his 20th pro season.

"As we were driving on that last drive it seemed like it was destiny – for us," Favre told ESPN. "I was so close, so close to getting these guys to the Super Bowl. I owe it to this organization to give it one more try."[cvi]

Too bad his last hurrah in the NFL would not be as rosy as it was in 2009. The Vikings were far from being a playoff team in the 2010 NFL season. They lost five of their first seven games. Favre was below average. He had more interceptions (11) than he had touchdowns (seven) in those seven contests.[cvii]

Despite the Vikings' horrific start, Favre continued to pile up on the accolades.

Favre connected on 14 of 34 passes for 264 yards, three touchdowns, and one interception in a heart-breaking 29-20 loss to the New York Jets – his former team – on Monday Night Football on October 11, 2010. He threw a late interception to Jets safety Dwight Lowery, who ran the ball back for a touchdown to seal his team's victory. Favre also fumbled twice in the early going. It resulted in a 12-0 Jets lead. Nonetheless, Favre earned the distinction of being the only player to have thrown 500 passes and 70,000 yards in a career.[cviii]

Minnesota finally got on the win column for the third time when they beat the Arizona Cardinals in overtime on November 7, 2010, 27-24. Favre threw for a career-best 446 yards to go along with two touchdowns and two picks in the win. It was his first 400-yard performance since December 5, 1993. On that day, he recorded 402 yards in a Green Bay Packers win over the Chicago Bears at Soldier Field. According to ESPN, the 16 years and 337 days it took Favre to replicate the feat "is the longest gap in NFL history."[cix] Favre also helped Minnesota overcome a late 14-point deficit to win on Ryan Longwell's 35-yard field goal in overtime.

A month later, Favre saw his 321-game streak as a starter (including the postseason) jeopardized when Buffalo Bills linebacker Arthur Moats hit him on the Vikings' first series. Favre suffered a sprained sternoclavicular joint in his right shoulder, per ESPN.[cx] His backup, Tarvaris Jackson, stepped in and threw two touchdown passes to Sidney Rice in the Vikings' 38-14 win over the 2-10 Bills. Favre didn't suit up in the game against the Week 14 game against the New York Giants on December 13, 2010. His 321-game streak as a starting quarterback had ended.

Favre's injury woes continued. He suffered a concussion after Chicago Bears defensive end Corey Wootton sacked him in the second quarter of the Vikings' 40-14 loss to their NFC North rivals on December 20, 2010.[cxi] Favre connected on five of seven passes for 63 yards in what turned out to be his final NFL game.

Favre announced his retirement on January 17, 2011. According to two team sources who spoke to FOX Sports' Alex Marvez, Favre had filed his retirement papers with the NFL. He had retired and un-retired on numerous occasions in the past, but it was official this time.[cxii]

Favre finished his 20th and final NFL season with 2,509 passing yards, 11 touchdowns, and 19 interceptions. According to Marvez, Favre's 60.6 completion rate was his lowest in five seasons. The Vikings also finished with a 6-10 win-loss record – dead last in the NFC North. They missed the postseason for the first time in three years.

A bruised and battered Brett Lorenzo Favre had decided to hang up his cleats after 20 years in the professional ranks. He had achieved many goals which countless other quarterbacks had failed to accomplish. He was already 41 years old. He had tried to win another Super Bowl title to no avail. Nonetheless, his legacy will live on in the hearts of many football fans the world over.

2015 Induction into Green Bay Packers Hall of Fame, Jersey Retirement Ceremony and 2016 Induction into Pro Football Hall of Fame

Even though Brett Lorenzo Favre started his illustrious NFL career with the Atlanta Falcons in 1991 and ended it in 2010 with the Minnesota Vikings, he was very much a Green Bay Packer at heart, no question. After all, he spent 17 of his 20 years in the NFL in frigid Green Bay, Wisconsin.

The Packers went all out in making Brett Favre a permanent part of their team's history in 2015 – five years after he retired from the National Football League.

On July 18 of that year, they inducted him into the Packers Hall of Fame, per FOX Sports' Sid Saraf.[cxiii] He soaked in the Cheeseheads' adulation before a sellout crowd at Lambeau Field. They chanted "MVP!" for five full minutes as he made his way out of the tunnel. Favre, who was accustomed to playing before thousands of spectators every Sunday, felt like a fan. He mumbled "wow" to himself several times.

"This is absolutely amazing," he told the fans at Lambeau Field, per Saraf. "If there were any doubts before, there aren't any (now). I truly thank you. I'm a little bit embarrassed that all this is for me. I really am. I never dreamed of standing here before you in a moment like this. It's just way beyond what I've dreamed of. I'm so honored."

"I want you to know I celebrate this with you," he continued. "We did it together."

Favre continued to deflect praise as his speech wore on. He said it was not just about him; it was all about him, the organization, and the fans. He then went to the Lambeau Field tunnel and through a set of double doors. He stumbled upon the locker room which had been a big part of his life as an NFL quarterback.

"It was like I never left," he told FOX Sports.

Moments later, Green Bay Packers Hall of Fame president Perry Kidder congratulated Favre. The former gave him the iconic quarterback a ring and bronze football. Packers fans stood up and chanted "MVP!" once again, per Saraf.

His former head coach, Mike Holmgren, and former general manager, Ron Wolf (the man who acquired him a trade with the Atlanta Falcons in 1992), were on hand. Holmgren compared Favre to a son he never had. For his part, Wolf declared Favre the best to don Packers Green and Gold.

On Thanksgiving Day, the Packers unveiled his retired No. 4 jersey in the north end zone of Lambeau Field during an emotional halftime ceremony during a game against the Chicago Bears. Favre became just the sixth Packers player in franchise history to have his jersey number retired (the others were Tony Canadeo, Don Hutson, Bart Starr, Ray Nitschke, and Reggie White), per ESPN's Jason Wilde. Green Bay Mayor Jim Schmitt also presented Favre with a key to the city several hours before the game.[cxiv]

Favre used the essence of Thanksgiving as one of the key points in his speech to the adoring Packers faithful at Lambeau Field.

"I know we have to be quick, we have to finish this game, but it is Thanksgiving, and we have so much to be thankful for," Favre said, per Wilde. "And as I think back to our time here in Green Bay, I certainly thank God for the opportunity to play a game I love and play it for a long time and in the best place to play football in the world."

"I guess the point in all that, it's pretty amazing, pretty cool," he continued. "I never dreamed of the unveiling of my jersey. I never dreamed of the Hall of Fame. Granted, that's awesome. But I dreamed of playing. Very few people can probably say this: The dreams that I had as a kid, mine have come true and then some."

Brett Favre then received the penultimate honor of any NFL player. He will be inducted into the Pro Football Hall of Fame in Canton, Ohio on July 22, 2016. League officials confirmed this during the "NFL Honors" show on February 6, 2016, per NFL.com's Gregg Rosenthal. The other members of the Class of 2016 are Tony Dungy, Kevin Greene, Marvin Harrison, Orlando Pace, Eddie de Bartolo, Jr., Ken Stabler, and Dick Stanfel.cxv

Brett Favre had achieved every conceivable goal for an NFL quarterback. He is going to be a bona fide Pro Football Hall of Famer. It is undoubtedly the most significant achievement of his career.

Chapter 5: Brett Favre's Personal Life

The only things Brett Favre knew when he was a child were sports and family. He finally broadened his horizons when he turned 13 years old.

That was the year when he became serious with Deanna Tynes. The two first met in catechism class when Deanna was eight and Brett was seven. She was older than him by ten months, per Deanna's autobiography, *Don't Bet Against Me!*[cxvi]

In 1983, they were at a party Irvin and Bonita Favre organized for the 17th birthday of their son, Scott. When the teens went on their ways a few hours later, Brett spotted Deanna playing basketball outside. According to Koestler-Grack, she was "a feisty guard on the girls' basketball team." It seems Brett Lorenzo Farve had met his match.

Brett already knew who Deanna was. However, they did not know each other personally. He summoned enough courage to approach her. He struck up a conversation while he ate a hot dog. The conversation started off slowly. It picked up when they began discussing their similar interests, namely sports. Both of them were athletes – Brett starred in football and baseball while Deanna excelled in basketball, softball, and karate. Talking about sports came naturally to both of them. Brett then displayed his athletic abilities by dunking the basketball in front of Deanna, per Koestler-Grack.

Scott and his girlfriend invited Brett and Deanna to join them for a drive. They wound up at the local cemetery. Brett managed to hold Deanna's hand for about five seconds. He even stole a kiss from her. He was that fast.

Later that weekend, Brett called her up. He summoned enough courage to ask her out while his brothers motivated him. She relented and said "yes." They would talk on the phone almost every night since, per her autobiography.

Koestler-Grack said their first real date occurred at a dance in Dedeaux, Miss. The couple enjoyed its first dance to a Debarge song entitled "Time Will Reveal." They were inseparable since then. Deanna Favre said Brett was entirely different from the boyfriends of her girlfriends – he would buy her sports items for their dates. For instance, he bought her a catcher's mask and mitt so she could help him while he practiced pitching. Irvin

Favre would complain and tell Brett he couldn't throw that hard to a girl. His son did not mind. He knew Deanna could catch the baseball although she did not say her hand was on fire. Brett and his brothers also often dived from the roof of the pool house and into the swimming pool. One time, she was curious and climbed on top. Next thing she knew, they had grabbed her by the arms, and they all dived into the pool right below. She was thankful she survived that ordeal, per her autobiography.

When they went to college (she enrolled at Pearl River Community College while he enrolled at the University of Southern Mississippi), they saw each other often because their schools were just 40 miles apart. They had their share of trials during this time. They even broke up once – Deanna ignored Brett for a month. However, he called her up after five weeks. They made up when he showed up at her doorstep before a movie date carrying plastic flowers. Brett never brought her flowers before, and that gesture touched Deanna all the more.

In the summer when Deanna was about to transfer from junior college to the University of Southern Mississippi, she found out she was pregnant. She was 19 years old while he was 18 years old. They decided to keep the baby.

"I'm not going to get married because I have to get married," Deanna Favre said in her book, *Don't Bet Against Me!* "And I'm not going to have an abortion. I made a bad choice, and for every choice there's a consequence. So I'm going to deal with the consequences, and I'm going to have this baby."

With that, their daughter, Brittany Nicole, was born on February 6, 1989. She weighed seven lbs. and two oz. Deanna liked her nickname "Britt" because it sounded almost the same as "Brett."

Brett and Deanna got married at St. Agnes Catholic Church in Green Bay, Wisconsin on July 14, 1996. They tied the knot the day before the start of Green Bay Packers training camp. They decided to spend their honeymoon in Kohler, a town just 60 miles from Green Bay. At the time, Brett was already in his sixth NFL season and fifth with the Packers. Less than seven months later, he would be a Super Bowl champion.

When the couple married in 1996, they wanted to have another baby so Brittany could have a sister. However, they were unsuccessful for three years.

Breleigh Ann Favre was born in July 1999. She weighed five lbs. and seven oz. Brett and Deanna decided to name their second daughter "Ann" because their mothers and sisters also had that name, per Deanna's autobiography.

Brett and Deanna saw their traits in their daughters, who could not have been more different. Brittany is more reserved and subdued (In her autobiography, Deanna said Britt reminds her of herself). On the other hand, Breleigh is the active one. She likes to dance and act, and she is also a cheerleader.

Brett Favre said he did not mind not having a son. Deanna wrote in her autobiography that people would have put too much pressure on a Favre boy. They would have wanted him to follow in the footsteps of his famous dad, a three-time NFL MVP. Neither Brett nor Deanna wanted that for any of their children.

Deanna Favre described her husband as "an amazing father" in her book, *Don't Bet Against Me*! For instance, whenever Deanna and Brittany argued, Brett would talk to their daughter in her room. He never raised his voice. He was the peacemaker in the Favre household.

"I'm amazed that the toughest man in football can be such a sensitive father," Deanna Favre wrote in her book.

Favre had always been a sensitive person off the field as well.

When he was a teenage baseball player in Mississippi, he met the disabled equipment manager, Ronnie Hebert. The latter helped Irvin Favre's football and baseball teams. While the other players felt uneasy around Hebert, Favre was not – he sat beside him at restaurants and on the bus. They established a life-long bond. When Favre already suited up for the Green Bay Packers, his wife, Deanna surprised him by flying Hebert in to be a guest speaker at a fund-raising event for the couple's foundation, per *Sports Illustrated's* Alan Shipnuck.[cxvii]

"That night is as emotional as I've ever seen Brett, aside from when his dad passed away," Deanna Favre told Shipnuck.

Brett and Deanna founded the Favre4Hope Foundation in 1995. That year, they reached out to underprivileged children in Mississippi and Wisconsin. Among the groups they support are the Make-A-Wish Foundation, Hope Haven, Special Olympics Wisconsin, Special Olympics Mississippi, and the Association for Rights of Mentally Handicapped Citizens.[cxviii]

The Favres encountered several tough times in October 2004. Casey Tynes, Deanna's brother, was killed in a vehicular accident on the Favres' Mississippi property on October 4 (Less than a year earlier, Brett's father, Irvin, died of a heart attack while driving). Four days after his burial, Deanna Favre discovered that she had breast cancer. She underwent chemotherapy and radiation treatment for the next four months.

Thankfully, her doctors declared her cancer-free in February 2005. She credits the experience for bringing her and Brett closer to God. She also became a spokesperson for breast cancer awareness.[cxix]

In 2005, Brett and Deanna expanded their foundation's mission statement to include support for breast cancer prevention programs. These include Ribbon of Hope, Pink Ribbon Fund, and Memorial Hospital, per Favre4Hope.com.

That same year, Hurricane Katrina – one of the worst natural disasters in United States history – ravaged New Orleans and parts of Favre's home state of Mississippi. His mother Bonita's house was flooded (Brett Favre had helped rebuild it). Favre used his Green Bay Packers press conferences as a platform to appeal for help for victims in Mississippi. According to Shipnuck, he had helped raise more than $1 million after just eight weeks.

For her part, Brittany Favre married Patrick Valkenburg on January 26, 2011 (they decided to wed on January 26 because that's the day the Green Bay Packers won Super Bowl XXXI 14 years earlier). They had a son, Parker Brett, the previous year. Brett Favre became a granddad.[cxx]

Unfortunately, Brittany told Bleacher Report's Mike Freeman in June 2015 she and Valkenburg had divorced the winter before she went to law school. She met Alex Mallion five months afterward. They got married in her sophomore year in law school. A year later, they had a baby boy, A.J. – Brett Favre's second grandson.[cxxi]

In the fall of 2013, Favre served as the offensive coordinator of Oak Grove High School in Hattiesburg, Mississippi. Under his guidance, the Oak Grove Warriors won a Class 6A football state championship, per MaxPreps.com's Stephen Spiewak.[cxxii]

Favre's second daughter Breleigh cracked the Oak Grove High girls' volleyball team in 2012. She was a freshman when her dad called the shots for the football team's offense. She has become an integral part of the volleyball team since then.

Regarding their faith, the Favres are Catholic. Brett and Deanna were married in Catholic rites in Green Bay in 1996. They are also members of St. Thomas the Aquinas Parish in Hattiesburg, Miss. Brett Favre was also a regular fixture at team Mass for home and away games when he was playing for the Packers.[cxxiii]

"He's faced some tough challenges, and he's handled them so well," Green Bay bishop emeritus Robert J. Banks told Catholic.org in May 2008. "He wasn't trying to hide from things. I admire how, in Deanna's book, he let it all be told. He went through the early part of life like a lot of our young Catholics, but it turned out well for him."

Favre has remained in the public eye even after his retirement from professional football.

He and his family own and operate Brett Favre's Steakhouse in Green Bay, Wisconsin. According to the restaurant's official website, it features his memorabilia and trophies from his playing days. Among the specialties include Jambalaya, BBQ Baby Back Ribs, BBQ Combo Platter, Chicken Florentine, and Bayou Pasta.[cxxiv]

During Favre's 20-year NFL career, he endorsed several products. These include Nike, Snapper, Remington, Sears, Sensodyne, MasterCard, Wrangler, and Bergstrom Automotive.[cxxv]

Favre has also become a key player in the sports media industry. Sqor, a digital sports platform, named him to its Board of Directors on June 17, 2013. He has been juggling several responsibilities with the company which includes senior counselor and product ambassador.

"I am excited to be joining the Board of Directors and looking forward to contributing in any way that I can to help the company succeed," Favre told MarketWired.com.[cxxvi]

Conclusion

People who hardly know Brett Favre may conclude he has had it easy: a legendary playing career, three NFL MVP awards, a Super Bowl ring, numerous endorsements, and a happy family. They may even say he is just a typical NFL quarterback who earned millions. Judging people on the surface is easy.

Little do people know Favre had to deal with many bumps along the way to super-stardom. He entered the University of Southern Mississippi with little fanfare. Nobody knew about him. He had to show everybody that he could play the daunting quarterback position. Once people had an idea of what his abilities were, they began to consider him as a good NFL prospect. Remember, Favre also suffered through a dismal rookie year with the Atlanta Falcons in the 1991 NFL season. A lot of first-year quarterbacks have been successful (think Andrew Luck, Cam Newton, and Derek Carr). It's somewhat odd to think that someone like Brett Favre got off to an inauspicious start to his pro career. But it's a fact –he did.

He was also lucky that former Green Bay Packers general manager Ron Wolf fought for him. If Wolf did not, nobody knows for sure how Brett Favre's NFL career could have turned out.

Even when Favre enjoyed plenty of success in Green Bay, he had to deal with the loss of his dad, several sub-par seasons, the death of his brother-in-law, and his wife Deanna's breast cancer diagnosis.

In spite of it all, the Green Bay Packers inducted Brett Favre into their team Hall of Fame and retired his No. 4 jersey. The Pro Football Hall of Fame in Canton, Ohio will also induct Favre on July 22, 2016.

There's a simple lesson which everyone can learn from Favre's life: Nothing comes easy. Every success comes with a similar challenge. Many people fail to withstand the storms of life. Not Brett Favre. He's had as many trials – if not more – than most people. He set himself apart from others because of his resilience both on and off the field.

It is the real reason why he will be a bona fide Hall of Famer. Thank you for being an inspiration to everyone, Brett Lorenzo Favre.

Final Word/About the Author

I was born and raised in Norwalk, Connecticut. Growing up, I could often be found spending many nights watching basketball, soccer, and football matches with my father in the family living room. I love sports and everything that sports can embody. I believe that sports are one of most genuine forms of competition, heart, and determination. I write my works to learn more about influential athletes in the hopes that from my writing, you the reader can walk away inspired to put in an equal if not greater amount of hard work and perseverance to pursue your goals. If you enjoyed *Brett Favre: The Inspiring Story of One of Football's Greatest Quarterbacks,* please leave a review! Also, you can read more of my works on *Drew Brees, J.J. Watt, Colin Kaepernick, Aaron Rodgers, Peyton Manning, Tom Brady, Russell Wilson, Michael Jordan, LeBron James, Kyrie Irving, Klay Thompson, Stephen Curry, Kevin Durant, Russell Westbrook, Anthony Davis, Chris Paul, Blake Griffin, Kobe Bryant, Joakim Noah, Scottie Pippen, Carmelo Anthony, Kevin Love, Grant Hill, Tracy McGrady, Vince Carter, Patrick Ewing, Karl Malone, Tony Parker, Allen Iverson, Hakeem Olajuwon, Reggie Miller, Michael Carter-Williams, John Wall, James Harden, Tim Duncan, Steve Nash, Kyle Lowry, Larry Bird, Jason Kidd, David Robinson, Manu Ginobili, Paul Pierce, Ray*

Allen, Dwyane Wade, Kawhi Leonard, Pete Maravich, Draymond Green, Dirk Nowitzki, Jimmy Butler, Marc Gasol, Pau Gasol, LaMarcus Aldridge, Derrick Rose, Paul George and Kevin Garnett in the Kindle Store. If you love football, check out my website at claytongeoffreys.com to join my exclusive list where I let you know about my latest books and give you lots of goodies.

Like what you read? Please leave a review!

I write because I love sharing the stories of influential people like Brett Favre with fantastic readers like you. My readers inspire me to write more so please do not hesitate to let me know what you thought by leaving a review! If you love books on life, football, or productivity, check out my website at claytongeoffreys.com to join my exclusive list where I let you know about my latest books. Aside from being the first to hear about my latest releases, you can also download a free copy of *33 Life Lessons: Success Principles, Career Advice & Habits of Successful People*. See you there!

Clayton

References

[i] "Brett Favre." EthnicCelebs.com. Web.

[ii] D'Amato, Gary. "Raised on Grit: Favre was Toughened by Brothers, Dad." *Milwaukee Journal Sentinel*. 10 September 2005. Web.

[iii] Koestler-Grack, Rachel. "Brett Favre." New York City: Chelsea House Publications, 2008. Print.

[iv] Gutowski, Tim. "Bonita Favre Tackles Questions About Brett." OnMilwaukee.com. 9 November 2004. Web.

[v] Peterson, Nate. "The Chronicile of Favre-ia." CBSSports.com 2 December 2015. Web.

[vi] Favre, Brett. Interview by Kevin Cook. "The Playboy Interviews: They Played the Game." Chicago: M Press, 2005. 155-175. Print.

[vii] Favre, Brett. "Favre 4ever." 3 October 2006. Television (via YouTube).

[viii] Montville, Leigh. "The Kid from Kiln." Brett Favre: The Tribute. Ed. Mark Mravic. New York: Sports Illustrated Books, 2008. 23-29. Print.

[ix] Wheeler, Jill C. "Brett Favre: Awesome Athletes." Edina, Minnesota: ABDO & Daughters, 1998. Web.

[x] Bennett, Chuck. "The Brett I Knew." Favre: The Total Package. Ed. Paul Kennedy. Iola, WI: Krause Publications. 2008. 19-21. Web.

[xi] "Brett Favre." Sports-Reference.com. Web.

[xii] "Southern Miss Football Timeline." SouthernMiss.com. Web.

[xiii] King, Peter. "Warmed Up." Brett Favre: The Tribute. Ed: Mark Mravic. New York: Sports Illustrated Books, 2008. 57-61. Print.

[xiv] Giardina, A.J. "1991 NFL Draft Day: Brett Favre Made a Bold Prediction." WLOX.com. 1 May 2015. Web.

[xv] Silverstein, Tom. "Trading Places: Wolf Hits the Jackpot in Deal for Favre." *Milwaukee Journal Sentinel*. 24 September 2005. Web.

[xvi] McClure, Vaughn. "On Brett Favre Day, It All Started with the Atlanta Falcons." ESPN. 18 July 2015. Web.

[xvii] "Brett Favre 1991 Game Log." NFL.com. Web.

[xviii] Demovsky, Rob. "Brett Favre Recalls Being 'Kind of Shocked' by Trade to Packers." ESPN. 12 February 2015. Web.

[xix] McGinn, Bob. "Aug. 6, 1992: Brett Favre's First Camp." *The Milwaukee Journal*. 6 August 1992. Web.

[xx] Demovsky, Rob. "Brett Favre's Best Packers Moments: His First Win." ESPN. 14 July 2015. Web.

[xxi] Demovsky, Rob. "Brett Favre Excited, Nervous About Packers Hall of Fame Induction." ESPN. 13 July 2015. Web.

[xxii] "Brett Favre 1992 Game Log." NFL.com. Web.

xxiii "Brett Favre 1993 Game Log." NFL.com. Web.

xxiv Garber, Greg. "A Brief History of the Lambeau Leap." ESPN. 9 January 2015. Web.

xxv McGinn, Bob. "Jan. 8, 1994: '93 Wild-Card Game." *The Milwaukee Journal*. 8 January 1994. Web.

xxvi "Green Bay Packers 17 at Dallas Cowboys 27." Pro-Football-Reference.com. Web.

xxvii "Brett Favre 1994 Game Log." NFL.com. Web.

xxviii "The 1994 Green Bay Packers (9-7) – T – 2nd NFC Central Division." Packershistory.net. Web.

xxix "Brett Favre 1995 Game Log." NFL.com. Web.

xxx "The 1995 Green Bay Packers (11-5) – NFC Central Division Champions." Packershistory.net. Web.

xxxi "World Champions – The 1996 Green Bay Packers (13-3) – NFC Central Division Champions." PackersHistory.net. Web.

xxxii "Brett Favre 1996 Game Log." NFL.com. Web.

xxxiii Silver, Michael. "Return to Glory." Brett Favre: The Tribute. Ed: Mark Mravic. New York: Sports illustrated Books, 2008. 62-69. Print.

xxxiv "Team Records: Scoring (Super Bowl)." NFL.com. Web.

xxxv "NFC Champions – The 1997 Green Bay Packers (13-3) – NFC Central Division Champions." PackersHIstory.net. Web.

xxxvi Silver, Michael. "Second to None." Brett Favre: The Tribute. Ed: Mark Mravic. New York: Sports Illustrated Books, 2008. 70-75. Print.

xxxvii "The 1998 Green Bay Packers (11-5) – 2nd – NFC Central Division." PackersHistory.net. Web.

xxxviii "Brett Favre 1998 Game Log." NFL.com. Web.

xxxix McGinn, Bob. "Jan. 3, 1999: Steve Young Ends Green Bay's Season." *The Milwaukee Journal Sentinel*. 3 January 1999. Web.

xl Silverstein, Tom. "Power, Money Lure Mike Holmgren Away." *The Milwaukee Journal Sentinel*. 8 January 1999. Web.

xli Nickel, Lori. "Holmgren Leaves for Seattle After '98 Season." *The Milwaukee Journal Sentinel*. 12 November 2005. Web.

xlii "Rhodes is New Packers Coach." CBS Sports. 11 January 1999. Web.

xliii "Brett Favre 1999 Game Log." NFL.com. Web.

xliv "The 1999 Green Bay Packers (8-8) – 3rd – NFC Central Division." PackersHistory.net. Web.

xlv "Brett Favre 2000 Game Log." NFL.com. Web.

xlvi "The 2000 Green Bay Packers (9-7) – T 3rd – NFC Central Division." PackersHistory.net. Web.

xlvii Silverstein, Tom. "March 2, 2001: Contract Sets Brett Favre for Life."

The Milwaukee Journal Sentinel. 2 March 2001. Web.

xlviii "Wolf to Retire as Packers' Executive Vice President and General Manager; Head Coach Mike Sherman to Assume General Manager's Responsibilities." Packers.com. 1 February 2001. Web.

xlix "Brett Favre 2001 Game Log." NFL.com. Web.

l "The 2001 Green Bay Packers (12-4) – 2nd – NFC Central Division." PackersHistory.net Web.

li King, Peter. "Finest Hour." Brett Favre: The Tribute. Ed: Mark Mravic. New York: Sports Illustrated Books, 2008. 80-83. Print.

lii "The Usual: Favred TDs, Snow and Pack Back in Playoffs." *The Associated Press* (via ESPN). 24 December 2001. Web.

liii "The 2002 Green Bay Packers (12-4) – 1st – NFC North Division." PackersHistory.net. Web.

liv "Brett Favre 2002 Game Log." NFL.com. Web.

lv "Favre vs. Bears Always a Mismatch." *The Associated Press* (via ESPN). 9 October 2002. Web.

lvi "Bucs Continue Best Start in Franchise History." *The Associated Press* (via ESPN). 25 November 2002. Web.

lvii "The 2003 Green Bay Packers (10-6) – 1st – NFC North Division." PackersHistory.net. Web.

lviii "Moss Grabs Nine for 150 Yards." *The Associated Press* (via ESPN). 9 September 2003. Web.

lix "Brett Favre 2003 Game Log." NFL.com. Web.

lx "Brett Favre's Father Dies." *The Associated Press* (via *USA Today*). 22 December 2003. Web.

lxi King, Peter. "Do You Believe?" Brett Favre: The Tribute. Ed: Mark Mravic. New York: Sports Illustrated Books, 2008. 90-95. Print.

lxii McGinn, Bob. "December 22, 2003: Heavy-Hearted Brett Favre Picks Apart Raiders." *The Milwaukee Journal Sentinel.* 22 December 2003. Web.

lxiii "Warner, Barber Extend Giants' Strong Start." *The Associated Press* (via ESPN). 4 October 2004. Web.

lxiv "Brett Favre 2004 Game Log." NFL.com. Web.

lxv "Packers Win Third Straight Division Title." *The Associated Press* (via ESPN). 26 December 2004. Web.

lxvi "Vikings on Way to Philly After Stunning Packers." *The Associated Press* (via ESPN). 10 January 2005. Web.

lxvii "The 2005 Green Bay Packers (4-12) – 4th – NFC North Division." PackersHistory.net. Web.

lxviii "Packers Rout Saints But Lose Davenport for Season." *The Associated Press* (via ESPN). 10 October 2005. Web.

lxix "Green Bay Packers History." FootballDB.com. Web.

lxx "NFL Player Passing Statistics – 2005." ESPN. Web.

lxxi "Favre Says He's Leaning Toward Retirement." ESPN. 31 January 2006. Web.

lxxii "Packers Sherman Loses Job After First Losing Season." *The Associated Press* (via ESPN). 3 January 2006. Web.

lxxiii "Mike Sherman." Pro-Football-Reference.com. Web.

lxxiv "Bob Harlan Regrets Making Mike Sherman Packers' GM." ESPN Milwaukee (via NFL.com). 4 July 2012. Web.

lxxv McGinn, Bob. "Jan. 12, 2006: Packers Find 'Best Fit' in Mike McCarthy." *The Milwaukee Journal Sentinel*. 12 January 2006. Web.

lxxvi "Favre to Play '06 Season for Packers." ESPN. 26 April 2006. Web.

lxxvii "Favre Takes Care of Ball as Packers Take Down Vikings." *The Associated Press* (via ESPN). 13 November 2006. Web.

lxxviii "Patriots Knock Out Favre, Right Ship with Win vs. Pack." *The Associated Press* (via ESPN). 20 November 2006. Web.

lxxix "The 2006 Green Bay Packers(8-8) – 2nd – NFC North Division." PackersHistory.net. Web.

lxxx "The 2007 Green Bay Packers (13-3) – T-1st – NFC North Division Champions." Packershistory.Net. Web.

lxxxi "Brett Favre 2007 Game Log." NFL.com. Web.

lxxxii "Favre Now Winningest QB in NFL History After Packers' Win." ESPN. 18 September 2007. Web.

lxxxiii "Packers Defeat Chiefs with 17-Point Run at Finish." *The Associated Press* (via ESPN). 5 November 2007. Web.

lxxxiv King, Peter. "Sportsman of the Year." Brett Favre: The Tribute. Ed. Mark Mravic. New York City: Sports Illustrated Books, 2008. 118-133. Print.

lxxxv "Manning, Giants Head to Super Bowl for Rematch with Pats." *The Associated Press* (via ESPN). 22 January 2008. Web.

lxxxvi "The 2008 Green Bay Packers (6-10) – 3rd NFC North Division." PackersHistory.net. Web.

lxxxvii "Packers Reach Agreement to Trade Brett Favre to N.Y. Jets." Packers.com. 6 August 2008. Web.

lxxxviii "Jets Set for Brett: Packers Legend Headed to New York." ESPN. 7 August 2008. Web.

lxxxix "Favre Throw for 2 TDs in Jets' Victory." *The Associated Press* (via ESPN). 8 September 2008. Web.

xc "Favre's Career Day Carries Jets Past Cardinals." *The Associated Press* (via ESPN). 29 September 2008. Web.

[xci] "Brett Favre Game-by-Game Stats." ESPN. Web.

[xcii] "Jets Continue to Soar, Send Titans to First Loss of Season." *The Associated Press* (via ESPN). 25 November 2008. Web.

[xciii] "Pennington Earns Vindication in Dolphins' Defeat of Jets." *The Associated Press* (via ESPN). 29 December 2008. Web.

[xciv] "Brett Favre 2008 Game Log." NFL.com. Web.

[xcv] "Report: Favre Told Jets to "Look in Different Direction." ESPN. 4 January 2009. Web.

[xcvi] Bishop, Greg. "No Tears This Time, Favre Says So Long." *The New York Times*. 11 February 2009. Web.

[xcvii] "Jets Give Up Favre's Rights." *The Associated Press* (via ESPN). 29 April 2009. Web.

[xcviii] Nickel, Lori. "Favre Signs 2-Year Contract with Vikings." *The Milwaukee Journal Sentinel*. 18 August 2009. Web.

[xcix] "Favre Throws 6-Yard TD Pass, Peterson Rushes for 3 TDs in Vikings Win." *The Associated Press* (via ESPN). 15 September 2009. Web.

[c] "Favre Throws for 271 Yards, Three Touchdowns in Vikings' Win." *The Associated Press* (via ESPN). 7 October 2009. Web.

[ci] "Favre Beats Packers with 4 TDs in Return to Lambeau." *The Associated Press* (via ESPN). 2 November 2009. Web.

[cii] "Vikings Take Control of Giants Early as Favre Throws for 316 Yards, 4 TDs." *The Associated Press* (via ESPN). 4 January 2010. Web.

[ciii] "Vikings Sack Romo Six Times to Advance to NFC Title Game Vs. Saints." *The Associated Press* (via ESPN). 18 January 2010. Web.

[civ] Rosenfels, Sage. "Raw Brutality, and Brett Favre's Class." MMQB.com. 7 August 2013. Web.

[cv] "Saints Seal Trip to Super Bowl After Favre Throws Late Interception." ESPN. 25 January 2010. Web.

[cvi] "Brett Favre Practices with Vikings." ESPN. 20 August 2010. Web.

[cvii] "Brett Favre Game-by-Game Stats." 2010 NFL Season. ESPN. Web.

[cviii] "Brett Favre's Late Interception Seals Jets' Win, Spoils Milestone Night." ESPN. 12 October 2010. Web.

[cix] "Brett Favre Delivers Late 14-Point Rally as Vikings Edge Cards in OT." ESPN. 8 November 2010. Web.

[cx] "Tarvaris Jackson Steps in for Injured Brett Favre to Lead Vikings to Rout of Bills." ESPN. 6 December 2010. Web.

[cxi] "Devin Hester Makes History as Bears Wrap up NFC North Title." ESPN. 21 December 2010. Web.

[cxii] Marvez, Alex. "Favre Turns in Retirement Paperwork." FOX Sports. 17 January 2011. Web.

[cxiii] Saraf, Sid. "Brett Favre Greeted with 'Absolutely Amazing' Ceremony at Lambeau." FOX Sports. 18 July 2015. Web.

[cxiv] "Brett Favre's Retired Number Unveiled by Packers." ESPN. 27 November 2015. Web.

[cxv] Rosenthal, Gregg. "Brett Favre Highlights Hall of Fame Class of 2016." NFL.com. 6 February 2016. Web.

[cxvi] Favre, Deanna and Hunt, Angela. "Don't Bet Against Me! Beating the Odds Against Breast Cancer and in Life." Carol Stream, Ill.: Tyndale House Publisher's, Inc., 2007. Print.

[cxvii] Shipnuck, Alan. "Sportsman of the Year." Brett Favre: The Tribute. Ed. Mark Mravic. New York : Sports Illustrated Books, 2008. 118-133. Print.

[cxviii] Favre4Hope.com. Web.

[cxix] "While Football Fans Count Brett's NFL Records, Deanna Counts her Blessings." SowAbundance.net. Web.

[cxx] Liza Anne. "Brittney Favre Marries Patrick Valkenburg." TheHollywoodGossip.com. 26 January 2011. Web.

[cxxi] Freeman, Mike. "Brittany Favre-Mallion, Daughter of a QB Legend, Creates her Own Greatness. Bleacher Report. 3 June 2015. Web.

[cxxii] Spiewak, Stephen. "Volleyball Standout Breleigh Favre, Daughter of Brett Favre, Takes Oak Grove by Storm." MaxPreps.com. 2 October 2014. Web.

[cxxiii] Kurowski, Jeff. "QB Brett Favre's Faith Made an Impact, Too." Catholic.org. 20 March 2008. Web.

[cxxiv] "Brett Favre's Steakhouse." brettfavressteakhouse.com. Web.

[cxxv] Sauer, Abe. "20 Years of Brett Favre Endorsements: A Scorecard." BrandChannel.com. 9 September 2010. Web.

[cxxvi] "Brett Favre Named to Sqor Board of Directors." 17 June 2013. Web.

Made in the USA
Lexington, KY
14 April 2017